S0-BCQ-387

AT HOME IN THE DESERT

Surviving and thriving for a day, a week, or a lifetime

Bradford Angier

and

Peter J. Whitney, M.D.

Stackpole Books

Copyright © 1984 by Bradford Angier and Peter J. Whitney, M.D.

Published by
STACKPOLE BOOKS
Cameron and Kelker Streets
P. O. Box 1831
Harrisburg, PA   17105

Photographs, including the cover photograph,
by Felton and Romaine Gamble.

All rights reserved, including the right to reproduce this book or portions thereof in any form
or by any means, electronic or mechanical, including photocopying, recording, or by any
information storage and retrieval system, without permission in writing from the publisher.
All inquiries should be addressed to Stackpole Books, Cameron and Kelker Streets, P. O.
Box 1831, Harrisburg, Pennsylvania 17105.

Printed in the U.S.A.

Library of Congress Cataloging in Publication Data

Angier, Bradford.
  At home in the desert.

  1. Desert survival. 2. Outdoor life—Safety
measures. I. Whitney, Peter J. II. Title.
GV200.5.A54 1984   613.6'9   84–39
ISBN 0-8117-2153-1

For Sally W. Whitney
who made it possible
and for George J. Sokol, M.D.
who made it happen

Contents

Preface

This is winter in another world. The wind has a wild, free whistle to it as it surges through giant saguaros, and they make the prickly pear and barrel cactus seem stunted. My palms enjoy the smooth, warm surface of a granite outcrop. Suddenly, the complexities of modern life are a long way off. Here on the mountainside it is as though we are first arrivals, a part of an orderly and harmonious existence as right as night and day.

It seems no more than fitting that our earliest civilizations emerged from such desert. It dominates our solar system, after all. Even on this planet, with its lushness of oceans and lakes and rivers, a third of the earth's landmass is arid, baking days and shivering nights. The southwestern desert of America's Sun Belt, happily, is not barren land that burns and blows, each cactus anchoring its immediate ground from the gales' scalding scratch. This last great frontier of our lower forty-eight states is more alive now than when Kit Carson made it home.

Our freshened night fire leaps at dry spruce limbs, as the first warm flush of nearing sunrise silhouettes on a high eastern peak a moving desert bighorn, the most coveted of this continent's four mountain sheep. Two great horned owls exchange their last hoo-hoo-shew-ho-hoo-hoo of the departing night, in which turkeys call. The tinkling sweetness of a rock wren joins the dawn-welcoming enthusiasm of finch, twittering mountain chickadees, and pigmy nuthatches who already are darting at insects, framing the lusty raucousness of steller's jays.

We eat the quail remaining from those roasted in the same fire the evening before with butter-dripping chunks broken from hot frying pan bread and sip our steaming tea from the cool lips of stainless-steel cups. We gaze into the ebbing embers of our campfire away from which a plodding desert tortoise veers. A small herd of javelina make no secret of their taste for prickly pear pads.

Hare are everywhere, from the desert cottontails of the lower levels to the eastern cottontails, one of which we'd startled into hopping two days ago more than eight thousand feet up a mountain. Cliff chipmunks chattered among the oaks and pines during our climb, alerting mule deer as well as a whitetail and turning a badger back into its burrow.

Now a bobcat calls somewhere deep in the bush. Presently, like a sough of air across the sand, there breathes a sound—softly, hesitantly, sadly at first, soaring and falling and lifting again—a coyote singing of love, of the magnificence of the silent places, and of freeness. Over and over again the gray canine howls, so tenderly, sweetly, yearningly. Then we are alone with the stillness.

These deserts are here because at the equator heated air rises, loses its dampness as it cools, and broadens toward the North and South Poles. In the horse latitudes, the area sandwiched between 15° and 30° north and south, it sinks and warms again, keeping clouds and rain from forming, and making instead parched, globe-girdling, parallel bands. In the portion here in our southwestern Sun Belt, four major deserts assemble.

The Chihuahuan Desert, with its succulent-leaved yucca and small cactus and intermingling spiny shrubs, stretches its winter coolness and summer rains from New Mexico down across the high and wide flatness of northern Mexico.

Melting snow joins both winter and summer rainfall to water the lofty and cool Great Basin Desert in Utah and Nevada, with its frigid winters and low profile of unassuming low shrubs, saltbrush, and sage with its insistent aroma.

The Mojave Desert, just below in southern Nevada, has its own chilly winters. It's then that most of the annual precipitation brings its gift of rejuvenating vigor to such as creosote brush and the giant yucca and joshua trees that make its higher elevations notably picturesque.

The Sonoran Desert embellishes Arizona. A relatively lush insert between the Mojave with its winter rains and the Chihuahuan with its summer storms, it shares the seasonal moisture of both. This and mild winters make it the richest of all four deserts in land cover. Over this desert, towering pillars of saguaro cactus stand their dramatic watch. Rainfall is so distributed some years that the Sonoran is brilliant with flowers more months than not, and yet the total moisture scarcely diminishes the cheerfulness of more annual sunshine than anywhere else in the nation.

Does this country call you, too? Come with us into it. Let us talk together of how to live where the silent sand sings.

My collaborator and I have had much the same experiences, and this in a way is responsible for this book. We both grew up in New England. Although we never met there, our schools were nearby, Pete's Dartmouth College on the second occasion being within a dozen miles of my Kimball Union Academy. We both fell irretrievably under the spell of the quiet beauty and peace of the mountains and lakes and forests where we built our campfires.

Their ever deepening influence was a factor that led us westward toward lives of action in the silent places, though it was symptomatic. Underneath it all was receptivity to an atavistic urge. The trail Pete followed was southwest into the glorious unpeopled vastness of the Sun Belt's deserts. Mine was northwest to the subarctic wilderness.

"There is a drama to the open spaces of the world—the peaks, the ocean, the desert—that calls to all of us. Sally and I happen to respond to the desert," Dr. Peter Whitney says. "We came, not so much leaving the East, but seeking the optimistic, open, and outdoor way of life that today causes people to wear cowboy hats, Levis, and rancher boots in New England.

"When I was growing up, hunting, fishing, riding horses, cabin camping, and sailing were among my pursuits. Sally went to various camps in the woods of New England and New York State. We both took up skiing out of self defense from the long winters. With our

removal to Arizona, we discovered backpacking. This opened up
new areas of the desert West otherwise not to be experienced.

"It also took us out of our cocoons of air conditioning and
motor vehicles and made us face the need to live within the hot
desert environment. Without that need, in the city you can escape
the desert almost entirely, and life can be very like the life wherever
you came from. That life is not necessarily bad, but you will never
know the desert or get anything from it."

Already the wind, having rested in the nick of eternity, is
starting to blow again, sweeping with it the fragrance there is in all
wild open country, including Vena's and my subarctic wilderness
where our log cabin awaits while we witness winter in another world.

I inhale deeply the same air eagles breathe.

BRADFORD ANGIER

AT HOME IN THE DESERT

1

The Dream Before the Deed

An old mountain man, Dudley Shaw, called it the enemy. Yet it is the desert's greatest gift. It is time—each morning's cheerful invitation to do all the things you've always wanted to do, your days no longer minced into hours and fretted by the ticking of a clock.

Doctors remind those who'll listen that human beings were made to spend most of their hours beneath open skies. With our appetites whetted by outdoor living, we were meant to eat plain foods. We were intended to live at our natural, God-given paces, unoppressed by the artificial haste and strain of man-made civilization—actually founded on the repression of the natural instincts with which we were born and which, so far, have kept the human race from extinction.

It's wasteful enough to squander the best years of your life earning money in order to be able to enjoy a dubious freedom during

opposite page: High in the Grand Canyon, beneath the open skies, and far from hurry and stress, you can sense the wonder and beauty of the desert, its mercuric sulfide vermilion eloquently blending with buffs and grays, greens and soft pinks and, among the chasm floor's own imposing buttes and peaks, mauve-edged golden browns.

the least valuable part. But by working at something you don't like to do? So you can live the sort of life you don't really want to lead?

It makes as much sense as the cramped existences city-bound millions are settling for, making themselves sick that they may lay up something against a sick day. Their worries and stress get to be a well-nigh incurable disease.

Yet the majority of people, foraging for their food in the crowded markets rather than in the free outdoors, believe that today they have no other choice.

Air Castles

But there still are pathless places. There are regions right now where the "good old days" many dream about continue to exist, some of them better than ever.

What about you? Would you like to get away from the concrete cliffs and the asphalt jungles? Would you prefer, in exchange, wind-heaving stillness in which coyotes some nights yip yearningly of love? Instead of inhaling day after day the poisonous fumes that smear traffic's relentless din, would you rather breathe the same air that here the golden and bald eagles breathe?

A while ago, we decided we would, and now we do. One of us has relished uninterrupted year after year of desert living. The other has found living part of the time in the desert and the remainder in the Far North more satisfying because of the contrast.

The Sun Belt's southwestern desert—the sunny solitudes embellishing Arizona, Utah, Nevada, and the state of New Mexico with its Old World charm—is still as exciting and enviable for our wives and ourselves as that first glimpse of Mount Everest from Darjeeling's Tiger Hill.

If you have built castles in the air, your work need not be lost. That is where they should start. Now you can put the foundations under them. There are spots just right for each of us. Try one out for some holiday-expanded weekend, a fortnight, or those vacation weeks. It could be yours for a lifetime and mean happiness, health, and that route to freedom that prosperity can open by providing the wherewithal to buy it.

"If one advances confidently in the direction of his dreams, and endeavors to lead the life which he has imagined,'' Thoreau said, ''he will meet with a success unexpected in common hours.''

Half of America's Sunniest Cities

Does sunshine brighten for you the lure of untrampled desert stretches, mesas scoured by sand-sharpened wind, sere heights where even the cacti struggle to survive, and a lusty young trout stream rushing down into New Mexico through Engelmann spruce and subalpine fir to mature in the notable Rio Grande?

Then it may be important for you to consider that five of the ten American cities with the most annual hours of sunlight are in the Sun Belt's treasure chest, which this book stakes out. Tucson and Phoenix are ranked first and second, Las Vegas third, Albuquerque seventh, and Salt Lake City tenth. One reason the population continues to grow here in the land of the sun may be because a bikini takes up less room in one's travel gear than a raincoat.

Again Frontier America

Once again, for more and more people, the American frontier is in the West. The fascinating romance of this region long has been known throughout the world. Not as commonly known is the uncommon magnitude of natural resources in today's West, an area producing over 40 percent of this nation's food, 45 percent of its timber, almost half of its coal, and nearly all of its gold, copper, and silver.

Even more rousing, here where the population growth now outpaces the national average by one-third, are its human resources. Jobs are more plentiful here and personal incomes are growing over one-fifth quicker than in the remainder of the republic.

You soon sense the exquisiteness of it all. We feel it in the desert's coming alive in the balmy predawn. Others find it in the velvet bulge of darkness pushing up from the gorges and deep-cut watercourses, as if inflated by oncoming evening's first breath, which rattles the yucca's mature reeds. Clouds massing about encircling mountains exhale the soft luminescence of twilight.

With the sudden sunsets of these latitudes, a fragile hedge of

wind-trellised cumulus clouds above a darkly forested ridge blooms
with such color that even the darkening saguaros, there as if to prop
up the night, become fringed with glowing lilacs, violet, and a deep,
almost fluorescent, purple.

The day is going, you realize, and never in your life will there
be another like it. Blue, of an opulence most can't remember ever
before seeing, drenches the last flaring embers of the cloud-smoking
sundown. A yellow roundness of moon floats higher in the serrated
east.

Everything, the distances and the vistas and the fact that not
a thing intrudes about you but the freshening wild, free wind, brings
a sense of release in space. This, in turn, gives a feeling of de-
tachment from time. It is as though, from such a vantage, you should
be able to see the future you have not even lived.

Treasure There Is

Time was a commodity that, at the turn of the sixteenth century,
the primitive Aztecs were measuring more accurately than the civilized Europeans managed to do. It was no help, though, when they
were confronted by conquistadores expanding Spain's culture and
piety throughout the Southwest and, at the same time, expanding
Spain's golden treasure trove.

The New World warriors, though wielding obsidian-edged clubs,
put up small resistance when the invaders reached two thickly wooded
mountain ridges where Mexico City now stands. The invaders added
to their plunder great rooms of gold, so stunning that at first Cortez
scarcely noticed there also the splendor of precious gems.

Such richness still remains within this corner of our continent
for the finding. To comprehend more fully crude mining techniques,
spend an unhurried day wandering through the National Anthro-
pological Museum in Mexico City, in many ways the most eloquent
gathering place in our neighboring country.

Treasure There May Be

The adrenaline-stirring promise of buried treasure is also here.
There is a tale about gold nuggets concealed beneath what was a
cabin's stone fireplace in a canyon on the border of Valencia and

McKinley counties on the Continental Divide. And another about lode that the survivors of the wrecked Spanish ship, the *Isabella Catolica,* came upon in a vein exposed by erosion. It is reputed that the yellow metal still lies buried in Arizona between the Cobari Mountains and the Mexican border.

Then there is the incredible richness of some of Montezuma's treasure believed to be cached in Utah beneath White Mountain in Johnson's Canyon, more precisely about thirty miles from Kanab in Kane County.

Add to these stories the fact that nearly half a million dollars was stolen in fourteen years from Wells Fargo stagecoaches, offices, and other properties, during which time sixteen drivers and guards were killed or wounded.

Did the thieves, with posses just behind them, hide or bury the money? The occasional treasure seeker, hunting along the old routes, occasionally uncovers the concealed swag of fleeing train robbers.

The Mislaid Mines

There is always the possibility that you'll one day come across a long-sought lost mine, although Mark Twain did note, "A mine is a hole in the ground owned by a liar."

Of the dozens of lost lodes that keep adding excitement to conversations, the Lost Dutchman in Arizona's Superstition Mountains, a bit eastward of Phoenix, still arouses the most attention. Jacob Walz, who first bragged about it when swapping nuggets for whiskey, started all the speculation back in 1881 and for a while heightened the fervor with more mysterious samples.

Sought also in Arizona are the Lost Nugget Mine, supposedly on the Colorado River's eastern side below Topoc and, somewhere above Yuma, the Lost Sixshooter. The object of other searches in the same state is the Lost Soapmaker Mine, looked for where the sun sets west of Ajo on the road once followed by the Butterfield stages. Then, supposedly, even nearer Tucson there is the Escalante, more picturesquely known as the Lost Mine with the Iron Door.

The Golden Opportunities

Thomas B. Nolan, head of the U.S. Geological Survey, wasn't forgetting the Sun Belt's ridge-and-canyon-scored deserts when he noted that ten times as many mining regions may remain to be found in this country as those already known. Furthermore, in his opinion, these should include again as many primary areas as there are already.

Burros now run wild and are protected by law in some areas here. Before, one memorably sought shelter beneath a certain dark outcrop in Nevada and so is credited for Jim Butler's locating the Tonopah Mine which yielded roughly $150 million in gold and silver.

With precious metal values where they have climbed from the world's fixed price of $35 for one ounce of gold in 1934, for example, both weekend and full-time prospectors keep searching with often gratifying success. You still can happen upon a silver, gold, or other rich strike while camping, hunting, backpacking, or just plain hiking.

In New Mexico, gold has been found in all the counties along the Rio Grande. Dry placers on both sides of the Colorado River in Arizona have been profitably worked with dry concentrates and vibrators.

The earliest placer mining in production of any note here in the Southwest was developed from diggings near Golden in Santa Fe County, New Mexico. These deposits were worked as early as 1828. The Carlin Mine near Carlin, Nevada, was opened in 1965 nearly a century and a half later. It is considered the largest gold discovery of the past fifty years, containing an estimated $120 million of the yellow metal.

Gold taken from the copper ore mined at the vast open-pit mine at Bingham, Utah, nearly equals the amount produced from the biggest gold mine in the United States.

Placer gold has been located along many of the intermittent and occasional streams of the arid regions in parts of Nevada, New Mexico, and Arizona. Some districts in Nevada are estimated to have produced a minimum of 1,700,000 ounces of placer gold from 1948 to 1968. The total output of precious metals in Nevada has been approximately $1 billion dollars, of which about 40 percent has been in gold and the rest in silver.

Dry washers have been used for many years in the southwestern United States where water is scarce, particularly in New Mexico where some millions of dollars of gold have been thus obtained.

Burros like this one still run wild and are protected by law in many of the Sun Belt's deserts.

Too, apparently unmined placer deposits have been come upon in at least six districts.

Many also use dry washers with success in Nevada and Arizona. Dry streambeds prove likely places to look, while throughout the desert the metal is frequently spotted where it has been washed downward and dropped by an infrequent cloudburst.

The Grand Canyon

Two billion years of erosion of less than one inch in ten centuries have cut through layered colors deep into a huge and dry plateau to make just part of the seventeen-hundred-mile Colorado River.

As far back as 1540 the Spanish had reached the Grand Canyon in their quest for golden cities and pagan souls. What they came upon were the stone ruins that marked the last trace of vanished populations.

Later gold seekers, American *gravel punchers,* panning and sluicing and also dredging, had little better fortune with the Colorado River down to where the Little Colorado meets its waters on the terminus of Marble Canyon. There the river veers west with no lessening of its walls to begin the Grand Canyon, scarcely intruded upon until John Wesley Powell brought his expedition there in the second half of the nineteenth century.

At Lipan Point, where the slash of sidal gorges on the Canyon's southern rim drop toward the Colorado River below, Major Powell penned, "We are three-quarters of a mile in the depths of the earth, and the great river shrinks into insignificance as it dashes its angry waves against the walls and cliffs that rise to the world above."

Even if the legendary city rooftops tiled with gold and streets lined with nothing but silversmiths' shops had been discovered, they would have been dwarfed by the Grand Canyon's own magic magnificence.

The Desert's Great Rio Grande

In epic persistence early in the sixteenth century to join their countrymen in the West, Alvar Nunez Cabaza de Vace and three likewise bedraggled and emaciated companions, the only survivors of a Spanish expedition that eight years before had gone ashore in what is now Florida, became the first known individuals other than natives to come upon the Rio Grande.

Though none of the Spanish ever found precious metals by the Rio Grande River, three centuries later silver was located in the San Juan Mountains at its headwaters. Prospectors in force were panning and digging and sluicing here by 1873. These days thousands of ounces have already been panned and dredged from its upper reaches.

The Thousand Ghost Towns

The ghost towns are for many worth the price of admission. There's the magnetism of Tombstone, that town too tough to die. In another, Skiddo, an already hanged Joe Simpson was dug up and dangled from a rope a second time. And there is Silverbell, called the hellhole of Arizona when it was booming.

Over a thousand ghost towns remain, four hundred in Arizona alone. Among these, Jerome still clings haphazardly to the slant of Mingus Mountain, some of its houses a thousand feet higher than its neighbors'. In another they'll point out for you where Wyatt Earp's guns dotted the rails of the O.K. Corral.

White Hills, now only a few deserted buildings, accounted for $12 million worth of gold when the yellow metal went for a lot less than it does today. There's no more than a scattering of traces of where Aurora sheltered as many as ten thousand people in early gold rush days. Only adobe remnants remain of La Paz, which in the mid-1800's was considered by many to be Arizona's leading city.

Virginia City, Nevada's most noted ghost town, is still a prime tourist attraction. The deteriorating foundations and the crumbled walls are all that remain of Hamilton, the hub of a mining area that is supposed to have brought at least $70 million out of the ground. Braying burros, as little bothered by such spiny fodder as the barrel cactus as they have ever been, are the only reminders of other settlements in other places.

"They were rough in those days," Mark Twain wrote. "They fairly reveled in gold, whisky, fights, and fandangoes, and were unspeakably happy."

Ghost towns are prime tourist attractions, reminders of other times and other people who learned to cope and thrive in the desert.

It's All Here

A golden eagle circles the sands on alleys of air. The atmosphere here is so transparent and steady that when American scientists, planning what will be the world's largest telescope, narrowed the suitable sites to two, Arizona's Mount Graham was one of them. Testing began here as well as at an inactive Hawaiian volcano. This nation's biggest solar and second biggest stellar telescopes are already nearby in the Sun Belt's southwestern desert.

Not far away, prehistoric cliff dwellings remain preserved by the dryness of the sands they overlook. There's the feel of earthly magniloquence, inherent in all such tiered mazes, where their dwellers thrived and one day vanished. Other human beings disappeared before in these sere stretches where now archaeologists find evidence of meat-hunting spearmen as far back as 25,000 B.C.

It's all here. A stillness of coyotes. Desert bighorn sheep gazing down at the fewer Sonoran pronghorn antelope in grassy lowlands. The stronghold of Cochise. A game trail embedded by its own weight in the yielding shoulder of an Arizona hill where Geronimo, too, eluded the cavalry.

Across from still more cliff dwellings in Los Alamos is Santa Fe, North America's oldest continuous seat of government. Grotesque charm in eroded spires. Crags autographed by mesa-leveled gales. Exquisitely hued petrified trees. Thirsty heights where even the cacti struggle to survive.

For the same reason Ernest Thompson Seton gave for writing *Two Little Savages,* his book about the American outdoors that helped us both grow up, we each write too: "Because I have known the torment of thirst, I would dig a well where others may drink."

2

Loafing Along and Looking

Henry David Thoreau, who said, "There is no remedy for love but to love more," realized from rather more experience that the cure for walking is similar. He once remarked that there was nothing he did better, likely because what he was really speaking of was sauntering.

"I have met with but one or two persons in the course of my life who understood the art of taking walks—who had a genius, so to speak, for sauntering.

"Some would derive the word from *sans terre*, without land or home; having no particular home, but equally at home everywhere. For this is the secret of successful sauntering. He who sits still in a house all the time may be the greatest vagrant of all; but the saunterer is no more vagrant than the meandering river, which is all the while sedulously seeking the shortest course to the sea.

---

opposite page: Pathless places beneath the clear desert sky are where nature intended human beings to spend most of their hours. Sauntering among the desert spoon on this hillside can preserve health and spirits.

"If you have paid your debts, and made your will, and settled all your affairs, and are a free man, then you are ready for a walk.

"To come down to my own experience, I sometimes have felt almost alone hereabouts in practicing this noble art, though if their own assertions are to be received, most of my townsmen would fain walk sometimes as I do, but they cannot.

"No wealth can buy the requisite leisure, freedom, and independence which are the capital in this profession. It requires a direct dispensation from Heaven to become a walker. You must be born into the family of the walkers.

"Some of my townsmen, it is true, can remember and have described to me some walks which they took ten years ago, in which they were so blessed as to lose themselves for half an hour in the woods. But I know very well that they have confined themselves to the highway ever since. . . .

"I think that I cannot preserve my health and spirits, unless I spend four hours a day, at least—and it is commonly more than that—sauntering through the woods and over the hills and fields, absolutely free from all worldly engagements.

"When sometimes I am reminded that the mechanics and shopkeepers stay in their shops not only all the forenoon, but all the afternoon too, sitting with crossed legs—I think that they deserve some credit for not having all committed suicide long ago."

The Ramble a Continent Wide

A lifelong taste for rambling, which Meriwether Lewis admitted to, turned out to be especially important to the success of the Lewis and Clark expedition in traversing North America from the Missouri to the Pacific Ocean across a wilderness that became ten states—opening the course through which a new tide of American settlers surged.

The Pathless Places

Pathless places beneath open skies are where nature intended human beings to spend most of their hours. With appetites sharpened by outdoor living, they were meant to eat plain food. It was at their own natural God-given paces, unoppressed by the artificial hurry and tension of man-made civilization, that they were supposed to live.

Homo sapiens was bred for the wind-sculptured desert, the shadowy canyon, and a mountaintop where the breeze blows free. Just the thought of the great calling ridges that rim the cactus and sand can cause the most civilized pulse to beat faster. A mountain lion crouched in a sun-yellowed tree, unseen javelina nearing a spring, and coyotes howling beyond the fringes of a small, bright campfire all have the power to make even the most carefully barbered nape hairs raise involuntarily.

The Why, When, and Where

Yet, why walk? Why not ride a bicycle or, for that matter, a horse? Many people in the Sun Belt's southwestern spaciousness, where these months the companionable four-legged mounts are more prevalent than during dusty frontier years, do one or the other and sometimes both.

But walking has an advantage, the intimacy of contact between you and the world beneath. Even the short distance from the ground to pedal or stirrup alters the perception, which the differences in speed further distort. In fact, what you swap off by walking is the ability to cover more ground. There are always the many who accept as their primary objective the challenge of distance pitted against time. There is something satisfying in proving to themselves that today they were able to go so far in so many fewer minutes.

The walkers have the feeling that these of their fellows would, at best, be only marginally happier under scattered clouds than under the roof of an indoor track. For these dissenters, of which we have to admit to being two, the main attraction of walking is neither exercise nor competition but the opportunity to observe what otherwise blurs sterilely past automobile windows.

The exercise is still there. The legs that get you wherever, not uncommonly in all-day rather than half-hour stints, contain the largest muscle groups in the body. Physiologists tend to think of them as a second heart. Walking is good for you physically, too.

With so many experiencing difficulty in adjusting to the relaxed pace of the time-rich desert, after years of the Outsiders' rat race, pinpointing certain ostensible goals more definite than those contained in just walking around neatens day-by-day living.

There are such an incredible number of intangibles. The first lies in the energizing clear and uncluttered air, which opens immense distances. A peak sixty miles away seems a walkable twenty. Any slight eminence in leagues of unfamiliar flatness becomes a spectacle usually worth photographing.

The Camera's Case

Photography is widely and justifiably practiced and, in much of these parts, almost mandated. One of us still keeps his Leica IIIC in a pocket and, in another, an E. Leitz Optical Near Focusing Device.

The other is as seriously interested in the Olympus OM No. One that he carries. Our conversations may be at times more intriguing to listeners already adept in matters of portability; exchangeable lenses; through-the-lens viewing; greater quality and flexibility; and the ready availability of film in the numerous speeds and nuances of infrared, color, and black and white.

Unfortunately, the contemplative part of walking diminishes when you start to view the world through the very many lens. Another by-product is that, if one gets too preoccupied in serious photography's capabilities, he or she can end up looking like a burro packed helter-skelter, what with the never-ending accessories the art encourages.

This is the reason photographers also lean toward becoming lonely. Companions become weary of waiting while you use your macro-zoom lens on that trailside flower and leave to look for blossoms of their own.

Sketching and Painting as Nowhere Else

Others have the talent and the desire to record with brush and colors. There are pocket-size outfits for water colors and acrylics, probably the two most portable wet media, and for crayons, pastels, colored pencils, and the rest.

Sketching or painting in any technique is a distracting way to get through the hot parts of the days when more sensible people avoid the sun. The established medium is water color for quick sketches, and we admire the individuals who can handle it. It does, unfortunately, require water.

What Sherlock Called Observing

Then there is that for which Sherlock Holmes himself used the word *observing*. There are all kinds of plants, animals, landforms, rock constructions, and the aging efforts of our eastern hemisphere, Indian, and European predecessors to look at, ponder over, read about, and go out and see agin. Geology, anthropology, ornithology, and antiquity become more and more fascintaing as one's own insight expands.

When for What

Hiking's *whens* travel in tandem with its objectives. They are limited by little except time, weather, distance, mental and physical abilities, and most of all desire.

Here it is 3:30 P.M. mountain standard time. The temperature is 108° Fahrenheit outside in the open shade. It will rise another degree or so before reaching the day's maximum. If we were going for a walk now, we would want to start in a place where the temperature is approaching 90° to 95° instead.

With a lapse rate of 4 degrees per thousand feet of elevation, this would entail driving at least three thousand feet higher than we are above sea level. This would mean a trip of about an hour before we could begin the walk. The nearby country (which fits what we have in mind) is pretty rugged, and there isn't much daylight left. Maybe it would be better today to continue what we're doing, and leave the walk for another day.

For certain, it is not the time to go to the Organ Pipe National Monument for a marathon run. Morning was beautifully ideal for photography, sketching, and thinking, but definitely too hot for strenuous activity in the open sun. There is a season for hiking the low desert. Summer's midpoint suggests shade, high altitude, and low activity. That some individuals do otherwise, out of what might seem to others to be misplaced hubris, is a personal matter.

To hike in the summer, and there is no reason not to, planning should take you to your chosen area before the day's peak heat. The conservative aim would be at breaking and resting during the torrid hours and, if the country were rough, setting out as soon as the morning had sufficient light for personal safety.

Picking a route that would afford shade when it becomes needed, such as a canyon's east face in the afternoon, also requires planning, along with sufficient knowledge of the proposed terrain or at least the ability to read a reliable topographical map.

The Larger Think-Tanks

Just walking along can also be a wonderously workable way to straighten out one's head, though it may be wise to go alone if you are dissecting a dilemma. The out-of-doors can do what no think-tank can accomplish—give perspective.

Weathering the Weather

Television can give you the assist of odds-on weather estimates for the first few days you propose being out in it. There also is radio's weather station, which can be heard on one of the compact, lightweight sets wired for this particular purpose and obtainable for about $12.

Current dust storm, rain squall, and flash flood alerts come with the overall reports that are widely available. They are also extremely important. Sudden savage downpours, dramatic in their brief violence, can inundate an unseen range miles distant, whose drainage system may include the harmless-appearing declivity where you are.

Summer is the wet season in some desert parts. Rains are much less likely during winter, and clothing to ward them off can become so burdensome that many backpackers settle for just letting their regular garb dry out. Although mornings may be cold, mid-days are ordinarily hot. What can help many saunterers and strollers is the layer system of dressing, which most hunters who keep at it long enough eventually learn.

Cache or Carry

Everywhere a lot of beginning hunters, if the weather is at all cold, start off in the chill of the morning in perhaps a heavy mackinaw. In addition, many so stuff their pockets and weigh down their belts that, particularly if they push through growth such as tamarack with its shedding needles, they soon look and feel like an overloaded Christmas tree.

They puff and grunt and perspire along in bulky jackets as they top hills and breast thick bush. Camera and binocular straps continually hang them up. The pull and strain of loaded clothing becomes more and more uncomfortable. The chances are that by now they would like to shed the coat, but they have nowhere to carry it.

All or most of this impedimenta is often desirable on a serious day's hunt. That particular system of carrying it, however, is unnecessarily handicapping and unduly out of date. The answer is to be seen among the world's most experienced hunters. The majority, except those accompanied by guides or gun bearers, tote such articles in a rucksack on their backs.

Once you adopt this method, the chance is that you'll stick with it, especially as after you have carried a light rucksack for three or four days afield, you will never thereafter notice its weight. All discomfort is gone. Nothing dangles or catches. Your belt does not restrict you the way it did before. Your pockets do not bulge or press.

As you warm from exercise, the layering system goes into action. Off comes the jacket or extra shirt, and into your rucksack it goes. If you stop to glass a likely slope or b'il the kittle, or if you begin threading along a windy ridge, there is your extra clothing to put on again. You can get at everything quickly, and the rucksack, which needn't be expensive or elaborate, is no burden at all.

It's the Easy That is Hard

We hike, many of us, to solve to our own satisfaction any otherwise inaccessible mysteries hidden in sands, canyons, and mountainsides seldom, if ever, trod on before. We go to relish the fresh air, the freedom, and the good fellowship available nowhere else, and to get far enough away from the noise, restraint, and crowds of the big towns to enjoy the friendship of the seasons.

If our travels are comfortable, so much the better. There is no reason they should not be. As the Hudson's Bay Company says after nearly three centuries in the farthest and most primitive reaches of this continent, "There is usually little object in traveling tough just for the sake of being tough."

Rough it, sure, if you want to prove to yourself the very important fact that you *can* rough it. One day, it's true, anyone at all may be thrown entirely upon his own resources and forced to get along the best he can. But as far as preference goes, roughing it is a development stage.

Once we've successfully tested our ability to take it and have not found it wanting, a whole lot of doubts and inhibitions disappear. We find ourselves realizing that the real challenge lies in "smoothing it." We come to appreciate that making it easy on ourselves takes a lot more experience and ingenuity than bulling it through the tough way.

The Buzz That Can Be Worse Than the Bite

The Supreme Court's William O. Douglas observed that horsemanship is really just being able to stay comfortable, unconcerned, and on a horse—all at the same time. There are occasions, certainly, when a prime part of woodcraft is when the ability to remain calm, comfortable, and at the same time unscathed in areas noisy with blood-hungry bugs makes life in the wild places considerably happier.

There are far fewer such pests in this country of desert and canyons and breeze-freshened ridges than in any other parts of this earth we have encountered. But at times in such serenity and stillness one or two winged biters and buzzers can seem to be a horde. Yet everywhere today we need no longer feel as helpless as we were on Canada's great salmon rivers such as the Grand Cascapedia and the Southwest Miramichi. The same thing pertains to the trout streams of Vermont and New Hampshire where we somehow managed to endure the hatches appearing as clouds that kept on swarming upstream as each new day progressed. At the same time we enjoyed what were and are some of the happiest weeks of our somehow fortunately very happy lives.

A great deal was done to neutralize these abhorrences during and after the building of the Alaska Highway through the more than fifteen hundred nearly unpeopled miles between the sparse scattering of log cabins that then marked Dawson Creek, British Columbia, and those others at Fairbanks, Alaska, in six months and one day. It was then that enough individuals able to do something about it learned first-hand in this practical laboratory that mosquitoes can be a lot tougher obstacle than even the subarctic's incomparable muskeg.

When, after fifteen years of more than ten thousand different experiments, the U. S. Department of Agriculture succeeded in developing N.N. diethyl meta-toluamide for the Army in 1954, a large bottle of the pure compound was sent to one of us to be tested at the headwaters of the Peace River. It worked, and the findings were that the less it was diluted, the better it worked. It was long commercially marketed, however, in insect repellents in which it was only a small part. Now Deet, as it's been long called, is competitively packaged undiluted. Muskol is the first with which we've become pleasantly familiar. It is in such full strength that this mild-smelling liquid is still by far the most effective.

Those Remembered Campfires

Where it's suitable when you are traveling light, an overnight fire is generally more effective located downwind from your bed, lengthwise to it, and about three feet away. Stretch your poncho above where you'll sleep to reflect the heat. Your little camp will then be ready for a relaxing supper and a night's rest.

After you have fueled up on grub, consider taking time to dry out your underwear and socks, which would be damp in climates where the humidity is higher. Don that extra shirt. Arrange your pack for a pillow if you want. Build up the fire with the bigger stuff so it will hold longer, and you'll make briefer and fewer the intervals in which you will be aroused by increasing chill long enough to lay on more wood.

Then lean back and let your thoughts drift as lazily as the clouds across the yellow moon. Cold may awaken you in two or three hours. Don't just lie there and shiver. Hunch up and lay on more sticks. While you're warming, absorb the night noises—the wildness of the echoes set vibrating by two owls' exchange of hoots, and the sweetness in a bird's call, like a moonbeam turned to sound.

Relaxing on the Rims

The climate along some of the desert's higher-ranging rims offers relief during the hot months from the swelter of the lowlands, and the noisome smells and grime and nervous vacation traffic of overthronged and overheated cities in the paths to the Sun Belt mecca sought by newcomers.

Anyone who has sat there at night by a campfire, alone in the welcome coolness of a breeze's fresh stir, speaks of going back.

Joys of Sauntering and Seeing

So it is that what some people call loafing, others find the most rewarding and enjoyable fun of all. When such realization steals unbidden over many of us is when outdoor walks are enlivened by motive.

Such an aim is the easy prospecting along the way, whether for gold or oil seepage or hidden treasure. Foraging for wild edibles. The pleasure inherent in a small, sharp-lensed camera. The exhilaration in recognizing rough jade, banded agate, sapphires, and surely fossils.

There are the clouds and even birds that spell out coming weather. Tracks, sign, smells in the wind. The envy evident in erosion, as if water and wind and time can be never satisfied. Icy springs. Midden heaps, stray arrowheads, clutters of tepee poles, Indian burial mounds, and the storied caves of vanished peoples. Quail skittering in the echo of an eagle's screech, sharpening other sounds of approaching night.

In sum, walking the day away can be an enjoyable diverting way to shed decision-making and enjoy this different and beautiful desert.

As is the case with all worthy things, it is in preparation that the difference between pleasure and pain ordinarily lies. Thoughtful selection of equipment, venue, companions on those days that company can enhance, and the choice of apparel in which you set out, all go far toward assuring the development of a new and closer

contact with your universe, while consideration of personal respon-
sibilities and safety can save others needless effort and concern.

As the days lengthen and grow warmer in spring and summer,
so do the early hours around dawn and the gloaming at sunset. Short
trips can be taken then. For the longer ones, drive to elevation and
pick your route to suit your desires. As the days grow colder and
shorter these winters in a different world, widening areas open up
for exploration. Then there's improving your health by exercise.

You may like to give it all a try.

3

Warmth and Water

Chittering birds cluster over water holes, their sound bringing fresh life to dawns and dusks. Quail wing and leg waterward in latening afternoon and again when mornings brighten. Swallows and the deserts' doves swoop downward in company to scoop up their beakfuls of moisture. Wild animals turn their browsing and burrowing toward such directions.

Water lingers below cliffs after downpours. It accumulates in mountain rockfall and in gravel spread into the valleys by seasonal rains. Seepages appear when an arid canyon erodes an encountering of porous sandstone.

Limestone and lava have their sparkle of fuller, more frequent springs than neighboring rock. Limestone caverns are often so embellished, mesmerizing enough to confuse someone with a flashlight and a spirit of adventure.

---

opposite page: In the desert, as everywhere, your life will depend on your water supply. If your only choice is river water, like the San Juan River in Utah, take every reasonable care to purify the water before you use it.

The Water-Food Ratio

The amount of water you need varies with the wind, the surrounding temperature, the amount of activity, and the state of your health. Your body requires adequate concentrations in the body fluids and cells to balance what you lose through the kidneys, intestine, lungs, and skin.

The sources of this moisture are what we drink and eat, even the driest of the dehydrated provisions. One gram of carbohydrates, about a thirtieth of an ounce, releases about 0.6 milliliter of water. Protein produces somewhat less. Your metabolism yields about a half ounce of water for each 100 calories of energy.

To assure sufficient excretions of body wastes, a pint of urine must be produced each day. Ordinary breathing costs about ten ounces of water daily. The bowels require some three to eight ounces during this time.

Skin evaporation, even on a day when you're taking it easy, is about three pints. Exercise, illness, or those searing hours in the sun can increase your water loss tenfold or more.

Individual Baselines

Determining a baseline is difficult. An individual exercising minimally and living in a temperate climate might get by with an intake of a little over five pints of water daily. Any increase in activity, of course, increases the requirements.

In an environment like the desert, personal needs rise to seven quarts per individual per twenty-four-hour period, if that individual is walking at night. A gallon of water will take a walker across twenty miles of desert when it's dark, but only seven or eight miles in the sunlight.

Several points merit consideration. The first is that the kidneys do not respond to dehydration quickly, so there is a lag phase during which precious water is lost as urine. The second is that it takes about 2 percent dehydration to bring on a significant feeling of thirst, so you can already be in trouble before your body starts to signal that all is not well.

With marathon runners in the Southwest, for example, the twenty-fold increase in sweating necessary to maintain normal body core temperature makes the race not only against time, but also against fluid loss. Not only is an athlete's blood sugar lowered in ratio with such extreme exertion, and his muscles more and more deprived of oxygen, but the marathoner also becomes dehydrated to a significant and occasionally lethal degree.

It merits mentioning (especially because the thinking was just the opposite when we were on school teams) that taking in water during exercise is not in itself harmful. Violent activities like the martial arts can cause tears in a stomach full of fluid, and aspiration of fluids into the lungs can come from the same full stomach, but the act of drinking when playing football and basketball and such does not itself reduce performance. In fact, performance suffers when 4 or 5 percent dehydration is reached, due to increasing weakness, lessening concentration, diminishing motivation, and spreading lethargy.

Adaptive Activities

What, then, should you do in the desert to keep hydrated and thus enjoy your hiking or jogging even more? First, prehydrate yourself. The short burst that you get from carrying water in your stomach is worthwhile.

Second, drink water every chance that you get, remembering the thirst lag.

Third, in terms of energy expenditure, the cheapest cooling available is when perspiration evaporates. The least expensive way to supply the sweat is to carry water. The cost in sweat for carrying water in hot climates is less than 1 percent of this water you carry.

Sweating, panting, and, in fact, eating all cost energy. The thing to do in the desert is to eat heartily *before* exercising. With protein costing more in heat production than do carbohydrates and fats, it is logical that a diet containing relatively less protein is appropriate before hot-environment exercise.

Given the opportunity, the body defends itself against depletion of its volume and changes in its concentrations of fluids and in the composition of these fluids. All this requires access to water, salt and other minerals, and certainly food.

The American Diet

The American diet tends to be low in fluids, but high in calories and salts. We need about an ounce of salt a day to replace what we lose even when relatively inactive. Ordinarily, this is supplied more amply than necessary by what we eat. Calcium needs come to about twice that and are as easily obtained. Under normal living conditions, in fact, our diet is quite adequate. But when exercise or injury intervenes?

Moderate exercise in a moderate environment takes some 18 to 20 calories per pound of body weight to sustain energy demands. The average medium-size male then requires roughly two and one-half ounces of protein to sustain his muscle and visceral needs.

This means approximately a pound of meat or its equivalent protein source, depending on the degree of exertion. The needs may well be somewhat higher, depending on how much of this protein is transferred to energy. With the increase of sensible and insensible perspiration loss in the desert and canyons, about 0.58 kilocalories per ounce is taken to produce these mounting demands.

The body answers to energy calls by using up carbohydrate stored in the liver. Once this quickly available reserve is expended, protein is sacrificed along with some types of fat as an intermediate step. Finally, under long-term demands for more energy than intake, fats are used. Yet even in the bodies of people who have starved to death, fat deposits are still found, showing that fats alone are not adequate sources of energy.

The 80 Percent Factor

One's body is already about 80 percent water. The average adult needs some three quarts more each twenty-four hours. Half of this is lost through body wastes, another large amount through the lungs in humidifying the air we breathe, and the final sixth in the insensible perspiration evaporated to keep the same body at an even temperature.

In a pinch, you can get along awhile with two cups a day, but what you lack now you'll have to make up for later. Dehydration of from 6 to 10 percent of the body weight will result progressively in dizziness, headache, difficulty in breathing, and a tingling in the extremities. The body takes on a bluish hue, speech is difficult, and finally the individual finds himself unable to walk.

Unless water becomes available, death follows. On the other hand, the individual who has just collapsed from dehydration normally can be restored in a very brief time by the gradual intake of water.

Fortunately, water is obtainable nearly everywhere, even on the deserts. This is all to the good, for although under favorable conditions you could get along for a month or two without food, you'd do well to stay alive much more than a week without water.

In the desert, as everywhere, your life will depend on your water supply. In hot, sandy expanses, you'll need a minimum of a gallon of water a day. If you rest during the day in some shaded spot, even if it's only an east-west trench (see "Coolest When It's Hottest," chapter 8), and travel only during the cool desert night, you can put some twenty miles behind you to the daily gallon.

If you do your walking in the daytime sun and heat, you'll be lucky to get that distance on the same amount of water, and you'll be in far worse shape when you stop. But whether you sit out your desert encounter or walk back to civilization, you'll need water.

When Water Is Plentiful

If you have plenty of pure water at the moment but may have little or none later, drink as much as you possibly can, short of making yourself sick, before leaving the source of supply. You should sate your thirst, for instance, if you have the chance to do so before abandoning a ship or plane. In dry country, start drinking as soon as you reach a safe water hole and keep it up until you leave.

All efforts should be concentrated on taking what water you can, even at the cost of leaving other things behind, before quitting what may be an isolated supply. Don't ration the supply later on. Opposite to the now-outmoded ration practices of past centuries, you should drink until you have reasonably satisfied your thirst. Carrying a round, clean pebble in your mouth when supplies are exhausted can help decrease the sensation of thirst.

Water is obtainable nearly everywhere, even on deserts. If you have plenty of water at the moment like these children playing in a waterfall in the Grand Canyon, purify the water and then drink as much as you can without making yourself sick.

Conserving What Water You Have

There are a number of ways to conserve the water you already have. A major survival factor is to drink your available water until your thirst is sated, as explained above.

By eating less, you'll cut down on the amount of water demanded by the kidneys to help rid the body of waste. In any event, don't eat dehydrated foods and other dry victuals. Carbohydrates are best; 1 gram when assimilated by the body yields 4 calories of heat energy plus water.

By doing less, you'll both reduce perspiration and cut down on the loss of water through the otherwise exerted lungs. An important slogan might be: Ration your sweat but not your water.

Breathing through your nose and holding talk to a minimum both save water. Too, keep heat out of your body by keeping your clothes on. Clothing helps control perspiration by not letting sweat evaporate so fast that you only enjoy a portion of its cooling effect. You may feel more comfortable in the desert without a shirt and trousers. This is because your sweat will evaporate faster. But it takes more sweat.

Furthermore, you risk getting sunburned even if you already are what seems to be a good basic bronze. Therefore, it's advisable to use some head covering. Wear a neck cloth, and stay fully clothed. If you have any choice in the matter, light-colored garb reflects the heat of the sun better and thus keeps out more of the dry desert air.

If you do not have sun glasses, slit goggles can be fashioned (see ''Camp-Made Sunglasses,'' chapter 4). Stay in the shade as much as possible during the day. Sit or lie a few inches above the actual ground if this is at all possible. The reason is that it can be 30 or 40 degrees cooler a foot above the ground. That difference in temperature can save a lot of sweat.

Slowly and steadily does it when the desert is hot. If you must move about in the heat, you'll last longer on less water if you take it easy.

Clues Game Trails Give

The intriguing skeins of trails worn by the feet of passing animals can, and often do, make certain travel easier, as when we are looking for a gradual way down from some height. If we are trying to hold a certain direction, however, the safest rule is to follow a track only as far as it seems to be heading generally where we want to go.

It will be noticed in some regions that occasionally we will begin to encounter one game trail after another. In dry country, deepening ruts frequently indicate the welcome nearness of drinking water.

Water Indications

When you come across a palm, you can rely on water being within a few feet of its base. Reed grass is another sign that moisture is nearby. Arrow weed, cattails, greasewoods, hackberries, cottonwoods, sycamores, willow, elderberry bushes, rushes, and tamarisks grow only where ground water is near the surface, though you may have to dig. Purify all water from any frequented pools you may discover. Incidentally, small water holes in dried-out stream channels and low places are often covered. Search for them with this in mind.

The presence of other vegetation does not always mean that surface water is available. But the sound of fowl in semiarid brush country often indicates water is near, especially in very dry desert. Places where animals have scratched or where flies are hovering speak of recent surface water. They are good clues to where to dig.

Levels of Life

Water seeks the lowest levels it can reach. On the deserts that comprise one-fifth of the world's surface and one-third of its landmass, these often are underground.

If you're walking out instead of camping and signaling (see "Sitting It Out and Signaling," in chapter 4), if there seems to be no special direction to head, and if you can see hills, start toward them, inasmuch as the likeliest spot to obtain water will be at their bases.

Perhaps you'll wander across the cramped narrowness of a streambed on the way. Even though this may be dry, water can be trickling beneath the surface. Hunt for the lowest point on the outside of a bend of the channel if you plan to dig. The same general principle may be followed upon encountering a dry lake bottom. If the presence of water is not directly indicated by damp sand, try excavating at the lowest point.

Tinajas

Pools of water will collect in rock catch basins, called *tinajas*, that gather all the rain from the surrounding hard surface. These have been used by knowledgeable local inhabitants as far back as memory extends to supplement their water supply, because the same basins hold water year after year. Then there's the foot of cliffs with the occasional break between layers of bedrock that holds water at or near the surface, a possibility that the type and thickness of the vegetation can confirm as fact.

Solar Stills

The same sheet of plastic one of us has long kept folded in a breast pocket for shelter and other everyday uses can save you from expiring from thirst in the desert or at sea.

In the deserts of the world, with a six-foot-square or circular sheet of wettable plastic, up to three pints of water a day can be extracted from a bowl-shaped cavity some fifteen-to-twenty inches deep and thirty-six-to-forty inches across.

Place a cup, can, upturned hat, or other desirably wide-mouthed receptacle in the center of the hole. Anchor the plastic all the way around the top of the opening with dirt or stones. Set a fist-size rock in the center of the sheet so that the plastic will sag in a point directly over the container.

Heat from the sun will go through the plastic and be absorbed by the sand, causing the evaporation of the moisture already in the earth. The vapor will be almost immediately condensed on the cooler, underneath side of the plastic; the drops will flow down the underside of the steeply angled sheet and drip into the ready container. Capillary action will cause more water to be attracted to the surface of the sand to replace that which has gone, and the process goes on.

Two such stills will, when operating well, keep a man going in the desert, for when the production lessens after a day or two,

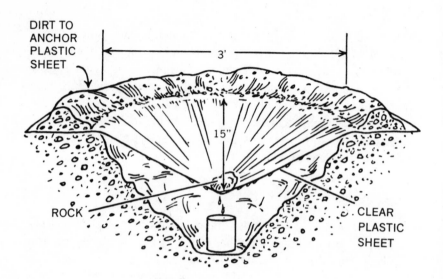

DIRT TO ANCHOR PLASTIC SHEET

3'

15"

ROCK

CLEAR PLASTIC SHEET

To make a solar still, you'll need a sheet of wettable plastic, approximately six foot square, a fist-sized rock, and a wide-mouthed container. From such a desert still you can expect to extract up to three pints of water a day.

the still can be moved. Production will even continue at night, though at about half the rate of the daytime flow.

Varying with the condition of the soil, the amount of water you can expect to extract in a twenty-four-hour day will be from somewhat less than a pint to three pints. But you can help the process along, particularly if you have selected a hollow or dry wash for your location.

You'll get even more fluid by cutting cacti and other water-holding desert plants into pieces and dropping them under the plastic. The rate of output can thus be increased up to nearly three times that of the sand alone. Too, even contaminated water such as urine, sea water, and radiator fluid not diluted with such a highly volatile substance as antifreeze can be purified by pouring it into the hole and allowing it to vaporize and drip in the heat.

What may be of interest some day when you're out fishing in the ocean is that salt water in the bottom of a boat can be vaporized and condensed in pure, drinkable form by this same method.

In any event, no matter where you conduct this operation, remove the plastic as seldom as possible, as it takes half an hour or more for the air to become resaturated and the production of water to start once more.

The Plastic Sheeting Preferable

DuPont produces a durable, thin, rough-surfaced variety of plastic sheeting that works well for such solar stills. Drops forming on smooth sheets do not have the same desirable tendency to hold on and trickle down to the sag where they will drip into the receptacle beneath.

If you're out with plastic that instead is smooth, carefully rubbing it to roughness on one side with the finest sand about can give it the desirable wetability. This side then should be put underneath when the still is set up, ready to help collect the distilled water and start it plopping into the container set below its lowest spot.

Barrel Cactus

The barrel cactus of the southwestern United States is another possible source of moisture. Acrid and mucilaginous, though, this

You'll get up to three times more fluid in your solar still if you cut pieces of cacti and other water-holding vegetation and drop them under the plastic.

can thicken rather swiftly. It is becoming scarce and should not be used unnecessarily but conserved unless there's an urgent need. Only then, cut off the top of the cactus and crush, as thoroughly as you can, the contents of the remaining section.

A barrel cactus three and a half feet tall will yield about a quart of milky, thirst-quenching juice. Scoop this out or suck it from a hole cut low in the plant. It is also possible to cut the pulp into portable chunks, to be sucked upon whenever you need more moisture. Discard all pulp rather than swallowing it.

Some other cacti, too, will furnish you with water if you'll mash and squeeze segments of them. The immature flower stalks of agave, yucca, and sotol contain moisture. If no flower stalks are present, the main stalks may be split open and this pith, too, chewed to alleviate dehydration. The root of the night-blooming cereus is also relatively abundant in wetness.

When Water Is Abundant Again

When water supplies are finally replenished, don't implement the natural-enough impulse to gulp down a lot at once. This is apt to cause nausea and vomiting. Instead, extend the satisfaction over an hour or two, starting off with a few hearty sips.

A barrel cactus like this one will yield a few pints of milky, thirst-quenching juice. If you cut the pulp into bite-size chunks, you can suck some moisture from them whenever you need it.

Is It Pure?

Although one is ordinarily able to get by awhile longer without water, any water with even a modicum of some contamination can be enough to weaken you so that at the very least you'll be unable to travel. It follows that you should take every reasonable care to make sure that the water you are drinking is pure.

The surest way to purify water before using it for drinking, cooking (unless this itself will ensure safety), dish washing, and such intimate tasks as brushing the teeth is to boil it five minutes at sea level and one more minute for each additional thousand feet of elevation.

Iodine Water-Purification Tablets

Chlorine-releasing compounds can not be relied upon in semi-tropical and tropical regions. Neither there nor anywhere else, incidentally, does the presence of an alcoholic beverage render accompanying water and ice harmless.

Water in these areas should either be boiled or treated with something such as iodine water-purification tablets. What the Department of Defense adopted is globaline, made by a division of Wallace & Tiernan, Inc., and sold at drugstores. Containing the active ingredient tetraglycine hydroperiodide, these small tablets have proved effective against all known common water-borne bacteria, such as the cysts of *Endamoeba histolytica* which cause dysentery.

Iodine tablets are more costly than halazone, but not necessarily overexpensive when you take into account their capabilities. Added to water, each tablet frees 8 milligrams of iodine, which acts as a purification factor. One tablet will purify one quart of clear water. Halazone tablets, used effectively for a long time in the cooler climates, also must be kept dry. The bottle should be immediately and tightly recapped after being opened. Avoid iodine if you are allergic to it.

The Economical Direct Approach

Tincture of iodine may be used directly in place of the iodine water-purification tablets. Eight drops of reasonably fresh, $2\frac{1}{2}$ percent tincture of iodine, employed as the above tablets are, will purify a quart of water in ten minutes. It is ordinarily a sound idea to let it stand twenty minutes instead, if the water, as it may be in the mountains, is numbingly cold.

Poisonous Water Holes

In the southwestern deserts of this continent a very few water holes contain dissolved poisons such as arsenic. You'll generally be able to recognize such spots readily, both from the presence of bones of unwary animals and from the lack of green vegetation. A good general rule, therefore, is to avoid any water holes around which green plants are not flourishing.

Avoiding Diarrhea in the Desert

Water is precious in the desert under any circumstance. Trying to keep up with perspiration losses is hard enough. Add to that a significant degree of diarrhea, and a difficult situation can become deadly.

For the desert traveler, the most common cause of diarrhea is contaminated water. In the United States, we are accustomed to taking a potable water supply for granted. Such confidence brings its troubles in most of the hot spots of the world. Even in our own country, it can be disastrous. Water from streams, water holes, lakes, and the like should always be regarded as contaminated. The back country traveler is therefore at risk and should be prepared to treat his water supply to avoid gastrointestinal upsets.

The cause of contamination is usually microorganisms from insects, the wind, decaying carcasses, and animal droppings, including mankind's. These microorganisms can be virus particles, bacteria, or protozoan parasites. The average individual will not have the equipment or skill to differentiate among the various causes. If you are away from medical care, there are a limited but significant number of things you can do to avoid or treat these sources of diarrhea.

When using questionable water, first take out any solid material floating in it. A piece of cloth can be used to strain the liquid. The best purification system will generally not reach the center of a solid chunk of debris, so it must be removed.

Next, boil the water. Five minutes at sea level is a starting point. Because of decreasing air pressure in ratio with increasing elevation, the higher the altitude, the longer it must boil. The common rule is to add one minute for every thousand feet of elevation above sea level. The boiling point of water becomes lower in temperature the higher the country, and it is the heat that kills the organisms.

Finally, add an iodine disinfectant to the water, and allow it to stand at least ten minutes. The murkier the water, the longer the iodine must work. Be sure to use a clean container, since it would be wasted effort to go through all the above and then put the water in a dirty canteen or pot.

Other sources of contamination are foods, either raw or undercooked that are holding organisms in and on them. It used to be thought that either cleansing the outsides of raw fruits and vegetables or removing the skins, would get rid of any such contamination. It now has been found that the contamination penetrates into the foodstuff for some distance. Overall, especially in tropical countries, as when driving across the border to fish the Sea of Cortez, it's wisest to avoid such foods from questionable sources.

Some types of diarrheal infections can be specifically treated in advance, so-called prophylaxis. Travelers' diarrhea is the classic example. This is caused by a definite group of bacteria. For short stays in countries where such problems are common, you can take doxycline (Vibramycin), one of the tetracycline family, beginning before you enter the country and continuing until after you leave.

Pepto-Bismol can also be used, but the necessary volume is in the range of a half pint daily of the liquid form. Such dosage also has to be carried on before and after visiting the questionable area.

For other forms of diarrhea, such as that caused by the protozoan *Giardia lamblia,* advance treatment has not proved to be a sound procedure. Treatment of your water remains the best prevention.

When Diarrhea Smites

If you get diarrhea, you will probably not be able to tell which kind it is without medical help. However, there are several things that you can do.

First, how bad is the water loss? Heavy diarrhea, which is mostly water and salts, will require replacement. This can usually be done by mouth by increasing your fluid intake. This nowise worsens the diarrhea. Indeed, you must try to keep up with the losses in a high heat environment.

Diarrhea that contains blood is an ominous sign. You should try to get help if you are in the back country. These infections are often hard to treat, so professional assistance is in order as soon as possible.

Do you have fever, chills, or other signs of systemic infection? Both ends of the scale tend to do this—the self-limiting viral infection as well as bacterial dysentery. Aspirin will help with this, but it does not treat the cause directly.

There are no specific treatments for viral infections. Supportive measures are all that is available. Bacteria may require specific chemicals or antibiotics. For various ones, doxycline (Vibramycin), trimethoprim-sulfamethoxazole (Bactrim or Septra), Ampicillin, chloramphenicol (Chloromycetin), or Vancomycin may be indicated. For protozoan infections such as *Giardia* or amoeba, metronidazole (Flagyl) is the best oral therapy.

In addition to this, there are drugs that suppress intestinal function. This is a mixed blessing, since it permits you to keep up with water losses. The losses tend to flush out the offending organisms, however, so that this treatment could prolong the disease. Our favorite remedy is codeine, which also suppresses coughing and is a pain killer. It is addicting, though, if taken for long periods. Paregoric and Lomotil fall into this category also.

Kaopectate can help. Some of the bulk laxatives, surprisingly, can help, since they tend to hold water in the gut. You must use your best judgment as to whether to use this kind of treatment, basing your decision on your water supply, location, time to definitive help, and other circumstances.

Basically, much of the problem can be avoided by watching what you eat and being careful with your water supply. Some pretreatment for travelers' diarrhea is possible. Many infections require vigorous medical therapy after they are identified. Being wary of the problem is probably your best defense.

4

Going Out and Getting Back

"A man sits as many risks as he runs," Thoreau said early.

The rest of the time, confidently hoping for the best while staying ready to handle the worst seems particularly applicable to desert living, although, for that matter, anyone anywhere can suddenly be transferred from the routine and the pleasantly familiar to the unexpected and menacing—even be thrust into a survival situation.

All such confrontations have a common thread. To a greater or lesser extent, the ability to control our environment has, if only momentarily, slipped from our grasp. It abruptly becomes necessary to do the best we can, with what is at hand, and now.

There is the old idea that though good judgment is all-important, good judgment stems from previous bad judgment. When serious predicaments are precipitated by the bad judgment in this canyon and sand country, one does not always get the chance to correct the original error.

---

opposite page: The safest plan of action when stranded in the desert is, many times, to remain where you àre, moving about no more than necessary and improvising the easiest functional shelter for daytime coolness and nighttime warmth.

The survivors are those determined to survive, particularly those with the ingenuity and the painstakingly acquired know-how to do exactly that. Whether there are certain circumstances when survival may be secondary to other considerations, each individual personally and sometimes instantaneously has to decide.

The passengers who stood aside and let others get into the sinking Titanic's lifeboats were not survivors but humanitarians. The survivor is the doe who pushes her fawn from the winter's last remaining food and eats it herself, with the instinct that has kept the deers' ancient breeding cycle alive.

Safety Is No Accident

This probably is as close as one can get to overemphasizing the importance of being mentally as well as physically ready to respond realistically to whatever necessities of survival come along. To put it another way, if you won't eat rattlesnake in a pinch, you may jolly well starve.

Many of the taboos with which we have fenced ourselves in by becoming civilized may one day have to go by the boards in favor of meeting the demands of a suddenly looming eventuality. Besides, rattlesnake meat is pretty good.

Minutes That Save Hours

A precaution taking minutes that could save thousands of hours of needless anxiety, effort, and agony is for each of us always to make his or her plans known before taking off into the desert and its ravines and ridges. If no responsible individual is thereabout, what we do is print this information briefly and plainly, along with the time, and leave it in some prominent and dependable place.

Even when we park safely off the macadam to rockhound for an hour, it only takes a moment to note this on the back of an envelope and secure it behind the windshield.

Among the fur traders who first ventured in much of the continental West, there long has been this tenet of the now three-century-old Hudson's Bay Company: If for any reason any member of this *Company of Adventurers* left an emergency camp, no matter how briefly, he was to leave a note in an obvious place stating in detail his plans and where he was heading.

Sitting It Out and Signaling

The safest plan of action when astray or stranded is, many times, to remain where you are, moving about no more than necessary, particularly if water is scarce. Improvise the easiest functional shelter if one is advisable for daytime coolness and nighttime warmth, and proceed as practically as feasible in attempting to attract help.

When somebody afoot first realizes he is unsure of his whereabouts, ordinarily he is not so far out of the way that he can not be located within a safe time or, if need be, relocate himself.

The real trouble very often develops when someone lost keeps blundering along, usually to his own detriment and to the increased confusion of searchers. Too many times he walks entirely out of an area, exhausts himself, and with his last remaining strength instinctively crawls into some dark cranny where not even his bones may be found for years.

The Downed Plane

Except when it is obviously only a very short distance to a frequented route or populated area, and there is a negligible chance of becoming lost, it's logical in most instances to remain near any plane. One reason is that, generally, it's quicker and easier to locate an airplane than somebody walking through the desert or anywhere else.

Spotting an aircraft can be even simpler if brightly hued and highly reflective objects are placed on and about it. With some aircraft it's effective to remove cowl panels and to place them with their perhaps unpainted surfaces upward to act as reflectors. Colored wing covers may also help.

When flying over isolated areas, especially in a private plane, it is no more than a conservative precaution to have along clothing, particularly footwear, that will enable one to handle himself most advantageously in the event of a forced landing.

In such an emergency, it is often possible to become generally familiar with the terrain while still airborne. To a more limited extent this may be also feasible even after bailing out; it is then important to establish, when possible, a line to the disabled plane if only because of its wealth of usually actual and certainly potential survival equipment.

In case of an impending crash landing, what can be all-important is to be braced at the moment of severest impact and not to relax at what may be an initial minor shock caused by the tail touching down. Actual continuous bracing should not be started more than a couple of minutes too soon or faltering muscles may be unable to maintain optimum tension.

A major hazard in many instances is that of one's head being snapped disastrously forward. One precaution is to swathe and cushion the head with clothing, cushions, or any other protective material available. Another, if not securely belted, is to sit with the back toward the front and the head held down by firmly clasped hands. Urination is advised to lower the possibility of internal injury.

Today's Automatic Pinpointing

"The development of practical aircraft enabled man to free himself from the gravitational bonds which lashed him to the earth which was his home," notes retired fighter pilot and present friend here in the desert, Lt. Colonel Frederick W. Brown.

"Wings lifted him above the desert, the canyons, and the mountains. An engine moved him forward over vast stretches of ground. He looked down and saw a new world. Everything looked different, and he began to have trouble—navigation trouble, how to determine where he was at any given time.

"Fortunately, in his search to develop a means of determining his position at any given time, he found that much had already been done. Ship navigation was fairly perfected by 1900. Dead reckoning, celestial, and terrestrial navigation already existed. So man, who dared to fly beyond his familiar area, adopted many of these positioning techniques. Today, with the development of radar and modern navigational air and ground instruments, a pilot can navigate over areas which he can not even see because of darkness or weather.

"Virtually all navigation now depends, partially or entirely, on some relationship between the aircraft and the surface over which it is flown; matching returns on radar, visual comparison with charts and maps, or on aircraft instruments associated with ground locator radio or electronic equipment.

"Today's newer methods of locating oneself are quite an improvement over those of times past. One of the two most improved are radar ground stations which can give you a position by having you fly a prescribed course, which they then transpose from the radar returns to a physical location on a map.

"The second is an interrogator ground system coupled with a transponder located in the aircraft. If radio contact between aircraft and ground radar control units is possible, a plane's position can be determined by having the pilot change the frequency of this transponder in the aircraft to a frequency requested by the ground unit, which in turn will transmit the plane's location to the ground radar.

"Should no radio contact be possible, the pilot may turn his transponder to an emergency frequency while in the air or on the ground. This emergency signal will be automatically transmitted to all units having an encoding capability.

"This signal is likewise automatically received by military aircraft, most commercial airlines, airport control towers, and ground radar stations," Lt. Colonel Brown concludes. "They will in turn alert rescue sources. As in radio and radar signals, this system is line of sight, and does have reduced limitation, particularly in mountainous terrain."

The Language of Symbols

Symbols designed to be seen and read from the air can be fashioned with anchored strips of clothing, or anything else usable and sufficiently bold and contrasting. Digging with its shadows, even scratching for that matter, will work in some places.

Any such marks will naturally be put down in as prominent and conspicuous a location as may be available. You'll make them large, perhaps a readily visible ten feet thick and, depending on locality and expediency, possibly one hundred feet or more long. Color can be vital.

An arrow with the point heading the way you intend to travel will indicate you are proceeding out in a particular direction. Perhaps you'll want the plane to show you which way to go. Then put out a large *K*. The pilot may take note by waggling the wings, after which he'll head in the correct direction for a significant period of time.

A long, straight line means you need urgent medical assistance. Two long straight lines denote that although a doctor is not required, you do want medical supplies. A cross is the sign that you are unable to proceed by yourself. A triangle: "Probably safe to land here."

You can indicate negation with a big *N*. Yes is *Y*. *L L* means that all is well. Are you hungry and perhaps thirsty? Then make a big *F*. A square will show that you would like a map and compass. Two *V*'s, one within the other, is a request for firearms and ammunition.

Aircraft Answers

Although responses vary, the plane can indicate an affirmative by dipping up and down the way the head is nodded. It can show negation by a slight zigzag motion comparable to shaking the head. The aircraft's rocking from side to side is an acknowledgment that your message is understood. A complete right-hand circuit signals that it hasn't been.

Body Signals

Certain established body signals will be recognized by many fliers.

Do you require urgent medical assistance? Then, as you probably already know, lie on your back with arms stretched straight behind you. Another widely used signal indicating severe injury is the crossing of the arms across the body.

Standing erect with the left arm hanging at the side and the right arm upraised signifies: "Everything is all right. Do not wait."

If still leaving the left hand at the side, you hold the right arm horizontal, that means you will be able to proceed shortly and that the plane should wait if practical.

If you continue to stand erect and lift both arms horizontal, you need either mechanical help or parts, and there will be a long delay on your part.

Standing and holding both arms straight above your head means that you want to be picked up.

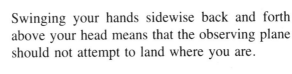

Swinging your hands sidewise back and forth above your head means that the observing plane should not attempt to land where you are.

If you want to signal the pilot where to come down, squat on your heels and point in the direction of the recommended landing place.

Perhaps you have a radio. If so and if the receiver is working, you can signify this by cupping your hands conspicuously over your ears.

If instead you want the pilot to drop a message, swing the right hand down in front of you to shoulder height several times.

To signal in the affirmative, wave something such as a shirt or handkerchief up and down in front of you.

To signal in the negative, wave such an article back and forth in front of you.

The Signals of Distress

The most universally recognized distress signals are based on the number three: three puffs of smoke from a daytime fire, a trio of night fires, three flashes, three shots, and so on, even to the three dots, three dashes, three dots of the long-familiar SOS.

Signal Smoke

The smoke from a smudge fire, improvised perhaps by adding green vegetation to an already hearty blaze, can be invaluable at times in indicating the direction of low winds to the pilot of a rescue plane.

Then there are the distress signals made by momentarily cutting off the smoke with a shirt or such and releasing series of three puffs.

Dit-Dah

Knowing a dot-and-dash code will let you send and receive messages with flashlight, mirror, whistle, smoke, radio, and numerous other devices including the primitive thumping of a hollow log. A mirror by day, flashlight by night, or by adequate radio equipment any time.

If you are memorizing the code, thinking of it as sounds rather than dots and dashes can save time. Then upon hearing a dit-dah, for instance, you'll directly recognize it as *a* without the extra step of recalling that dit-dah is really dot-dash.

The International Morse Code, which is the most widely understood, follows:

Flag	Letters	Intervals
right-left	A	short-long
left-right-right-right	B	long-short-short-short
left-right-left-right	C	long-short-long-short
left-right-right	D	long-short-short
right	E	short
right-right-left-right	F	short-short-long-short
left-left-right	G	long-long-short
right-right-right-right	H	short-short-short-short

right-right	I	short-short
right-left-left-left	J	short-long-long-long
left-right-left	K	long-short-long
right-left-right-right	L	short-long-short-short
left-left	M	long-long
left-right	N	long-short
left-left-left	O	long-long-long
right-left-left-right	P	short-long-long-short
left-left-right-left	Q	long-long-short-long
right-left-right	R	short-long-short
right-right-right	S	short-short-short
left	T	long
right-right-left	U	short-short-long
right-right-right-left	V	short-short-short-long
right-left-left	W	short-long-long
left-right-right-left	X	long-short-short-long
left-right-left-left	Y	long-short-long-long
left-left-right-right	Z	long-long-short-short

International Silent Periods

If you should happen to have a suitable radio, the most likely times to send distress signals will be during the three-minute international silent periods that commence at fifteen minutes before and fifteen minutes after every hour, Greenwich time.

Mirror, Mirror

A mirror can transmit a message by the International Morse Code or any similar code by using long and short flashes. More important is that the distance its flashing can reach—except when clouds, fog, or other thick weather has closed in—is limited only by the curvature of the earth.

A substantial mirror can be, therefore, reassuring enough to warrant keeping on our person whenever in the farther places. An armed forces Emergency Signaling Mirror, obtainable around U. S. air bases, is sufficiently rugged enough to leave stowed in a pocket, ready for any plight, when its potential may be lifesaving. Instructions for its use are printed on the back. A small open cross or aperture often present in a screened target area can facilitate aiming.

When you're trying to get the attention of the occupants of a plane that's no more than a right angle away from the sun, hold a double-surfaced mirror three to six inches from your face. Then sight at the aircraft through the hole in the center of the mirror.

Continuing to keep the aircraft in view through this central aperture, turn the mirror until the spot of sunlight reflected on your face in the back mirror coincides with the front mirror hole and disappears. The reflected light will now be accurately directed at the plane.

When the angle between aircraft and sun is more than 90 degrees, adjust the slant of the mirror until the reflection of the light spot on your hand, viewed in the back mirror, coincides with the hole and disappears.

Stop flashing once an aircraft has definitely acknowledged your presence, except perhaps for an occasional repetition if this seems needed for guiding. Continual flashing may be blinding to the pilot.

On hazy days a flier and anyone else aboard can frequently see the flash of a mirror before the survivors can spot the plane. So signal this way toward any plane you can hear, even when you can not see it.

By reflecting a flashlight, such signals can even be continued at night.

Instead of a Mirror

Any maneuverable reflecting surface, even if just a bright, peeled cactus pad, may be used instead of a mirror. This can be vital when you lack the latter. Heliograph signals of this general sort have effected more rescues than any other method.

A flattened tin can, or even the shiny end of one, will provide a stand-in. So will a sheet of foil. Just punch a small aiming hole in the center of such while it's lying on a flat surface, and use the whole as a substitute for a manufactured mirror.

The Way to Wigwag

Wigwag signals transmitted by flag can be seen for miles under favorable conditions, particularly if the sender places himself in an unobstructed spot against a contrasting background. Reading with the help of glasses, we have thus sent messages from mountain to mountain.

The flag may be something such as a large handkerchief or shirt, knotted to the end of a light pole some six feet long, so as to expose an easily distinguishable area. It can usually be most easily manipulated if the base of the staff is held at waist level in the palm of one hand, and if the stick then is gripped a dozen inches or so higher by the master hand.

All letters start with the staff held straight upward. The dot is made by swinging the flag down to the right and then back again. A way to fix this in mind is to remember that the word *right* has a dot over the *i.*

It will follow that the dash is then made by swinging the flag in a similar arc to the left and back. Throughout you'll find that the easiest way to keep the flag flat, for maximum visibility, will be to move it in tight loops. To send the letter *n,* for example, swing left and back, and then right and back. The easiest and most practical way to do all this is in a narrow figure-eight.

Hold the flag upright a moment to end a letter. Lower and raise it in front of you to finish a word. Swinging right-left-right-left-right will signify the conclusion of a message. The important factor in any kind of emergency signaling, however, is not correctness of form but common sense.

These Deserts' Most Prevalent Edibles

The major edibles in the southwestern deserts are the legumes, along with the cactus fruits all of which are pleasantly safe to enjoy.

In the summer when the young fleshy and thin-walled fruits are ripe, they can be despined just by the singe of a small, bright campfire, then handily peeled for devouring. The seeds of the older ones have long been powdered in primitive areas by pounding against a smooth, flat rock with a handily gripped stone. Some then are eaten as is.

The gruel known as pinole, made by mixing this powder with water, has sustained desert generation after generation since the first man and woman groped out of the dimness of a Stone Age cave. Important among cacti, too, are the newly green pads of the prickly pear, which are rightly familiar on tables once they are singed, peeled, and boiled.

The legumes are the bean-bearing plants: the honey and screwbean mesquites, the decorative Palo Verde, the tesota, from which comes the carved ironwood collectibles, and the Catclaw Acacia. All are small trees with fernlike leaves.

The Palo Verde is recognized by its open growth, greenish bark, and foliagelike feathers. Ironwood, growing dense and rough, becomes a large tree where its habitat so favors. Catclaw is a small, grayish tree, protected by the very numbers of its short curved thorns.

All have bean pods that, when green and tender, are sought for simmering and eating. The mature dry beans, like cactus seeds, are too hard to chew and must be cracked to be readily digested.

Interesting—and maybe invaluable in the murkiness of some muddled day—to keep in mind is that the plane atop a barrel cactus usually slants jauntily southwest. That of a single plant generally can be checked, for where an unmistakable and prominent barrel cactus grows, others tend to thrive.

Walking Out

If you determine your best chance lies in getting out of the desert on your own, travel only at night and in the coolness before the morning sun appears. Carry all the water you can though this may mean leaving something else behind. Stay in whatever shade, contrived or otherwise, there may be, and get your rest during the sun-blazing hours.

Unless you are heading for hills in the hope of discovering water, direct yourself toward a coast, a known route of travel, a definite water source, or some inhabited area. Along the coast you can conserve perspiration by keeping your clothes wet in the sea.

Follow the easiest way available. This means that you should work at avoiding loose sand and rough terrain, proceeding along trails whenever possible. Among sand dunes, keep to the hard valleys between the mounds or travel the ridges.

Except in coastal areas and those regions with large rivers traversing them, avoid following streams in the hope of reaching the sea. In most deserts, the area where water has eroded often leads to an enclosed basin or what was a temporary lake.

Always and ever give your feet all possible protection. You can, in a pinch, cross sand dunes barefoot in cool weather, but during the summer the sand will burn your flesh.

If a sandstorm blows up, take shelter at the earliest possible moment, perhaps in the lee of some elevation. Mark your direction with an arrow of stones or whatever is available, lie with your back to the gale, cover your mouth and nose with a handkerchief, and sleep out the tumult.

There's no need for worry of being buried by driven sand. Some old hands speak instead of the protection from the sun's shimmering heat that burrowing in it can provide in shadeless places. Desert survivors tell of inestimable relief imparted to weary tendons and muscles. Water loss will be whittled, too.

The Equipment Best Selected

An axiom to be followed with painstaking nicety when selecting equipment that may have to be depended upon away from the crowded places is to produce the best you can afford. A poor knife, for example, can be expected to weigh as much as a good one. It is very apt to weigh more because of extra material needed to reinforce it and as a result of ornamentation designed to draw attention from more obvious shortcomings. When we're really up against it for a blade, the supposed bargain may fail us.

"There is hardly anything in the world that some men can not make a little bit worse and sell a little cheaper," said John Ruskin, "and the people who consider price only are this man's lawful prey."

Cost can not, of course, be considered to be necessarily the final indicator of desirability one way or the other. As a matter of fact, the expensive extras sometimes supplementing otherwise functional merchandise may add unwarranted bulk and weight.

The soundest precautions to take when in doubt are to ascertain as many facts as possible, to weigh them as finely as we can on the scales of our own individual requirements, and finally to trade with a reliable and experienced dealer.

Camp-Made Sunglasses

A practical substitute for the sun glasses you may not have with you is a piece of wood, bone, leather, cloth, or other suitable material with narrow eye slits cut in it. Too, it is helpful to blacken the area around your eyes with soot from a companionable campfire.

Even though at the time the glare may not seem to bother you, it will affect your ability to see objects at a distance. Also, it can retard your eyes' adaptation to night vision.

5

The Mislaid Where

Somewhere in the shadeless swirl of the wind and sand, or during the quiet cool of a pumpkin moon, North stretches always toward the Pole. There is a difference, however, between where North is and where you are.

Yet where exactly is this North? More insistent usually, where are you? And which direction leads to that cooking fire you'd like to be lounging by near dusk?

Just as darkness is nothing more than the absence of light, and as no such entity as cold exists but only disappearance of heat, getting turned around is a negative circumstance. Individuals find themselves lost, if it does come down to that, not as a result of any actions on their parts, but rather because of actions they did not take.

The moment one accepts this fact is when all the strangeness blurring the strategy of orientation in wild country sifts into shadows.

---

opposite page: In the more open expanses that characterize much of the Sun Belt's southwestern deserts, it generally is much easier to keep track of your whereabouts than in wooded terrain where you can't get much of an extended view.

In its baffling place emerges the enjoyable positive, and simply resolved, problem of distances and angles. There is only one way to avoid, on your own, becoming lost in any canyon or desert. This is always to keep yourself found.

"It will give you a sense of complete independence and freedom of movement," notes a fellow Camp Fire Club of America member, Bjorn Kjellstrom, whose enthusiasm has been largely responsible for the popularity of the sport and skills of orienteering in the United States and Canada.

"Whenever you feel you can travel cross-country with utter self-confidence and unrestricted abandonment, you can explore far afield to find the hidden lake you may have heard about, the mountain glade, the waterfall, knowing your compass will get you safely and surely back."

The state of staying found need not be as complicated or confusing as it may first seem. Mainly it's a matter of alertness, common sense, and keeping a keen eye on where you go.

Human beings build their own bugaboos. One of these in particular blocks an unreasonable many from ever getting realistically started with this elementary part of wildcraft. It's the belief that some individuals are born with compasses in their heads.

No newcomer to the human race arrives equipped with an innate ability to find his way out and back through unmarked country entirely strange to him. This prowess is acquired. It is not instinctive. Even the most intuitive native, who has spent all his years in wild places, can find his way without some practical assistance only through regions with which he is thoroughly familiar.

Natkusiak, Mighty Pathfinder

Likely Natkusiak, an Eskimo companion of Vilhjalmur Stefansson during the dozen years the latter explored and lived largely off the country in the unknown Arctic, was one of the most celebrated native hunters ever known. As you may already have discovered from personal experience, it is difficult at best to get aborigines to accompany any outsider into strange wilds.

Such natives talk of danger from forces they might meet there, beings who torture and murder all intruders. They rarely say so, but what they fear is becoming lost. Natkusiak was an exception.

He had apparently developed the knack of finding his way anywhere at any time.

One day Stef's camp was out of meat. There was even concern about starving. Natkusiak started off to hunt. Eighteen hours later he returned, carrying the heart and liver of a caribou he had killed "far off."

The following morning he headed away with his sled to bring in the remainder of the kill, saying he would not be back for almost a day as it was a great distance away. That afternoon Stefansson went up on a hill about a mile from camp. From that lookout, to his surprise, he saw Natkusiak hauling a sled load of meat and actually traveling away from camp.

The Eskimo's wonderful secret for never getting lost consisted of always following his tracks back. On the successful hunt, he had wandered about without any regard to where he was going. It turned out that where he killed the caribou was within two miles of the encampment. But, unaware of this, he had trudged back along the same twenty miles of his curving and twisting footprints.

In that same way he had returned to the kill along the same slow, circuitous route. He was once more following the now well-broken trail when Stefansson intercepted him. The greenest of novices could duplicate the Eskimo's pathfinding prowess after a fresh snowfall, although it would take some doing on hard, bare, winter ground.

Where in the Sandy Spaces

The educated individual, though perhaps born in the city and a resident there most of a lifetime, can lead or make his way through strange country far better than an uneducated native to whom the same terrain is also new.

There is the rare exception such as the Shoshone girl Sacagawea encountered by Meriwether Lewis and William Clark, fortunately for the nation as well as for themselves and those others with their expedition of adventure and discovery. Read the histories, and they are fascinating, of explorers of other years. Listen to the intriguing accounts of this same breed today.

One reason for all this is the fact that knowing where you're going, being sure of where you are, and always having the certain

knowledge of how to get back is nowise a mysterious matter of
intuition and mumbo-jumbo. It is, instead, a positive and ever-
fascinating regard of distances and angles, where your pocket cal-
culator is a magnetic compass.

In the far more open expanses that characterize much of the
Sun Belt's southwestern deserts, it generally is much easier to keep
track of one's whereabouts than in wooded terrain where you can't
get much of an extended view and where each muskeg and glade
and green-bedecked hill looks much the same as the others.

This is offset to a degree one can not afford to underestimate
by the reality that the desert's unpeopled distances are so tremendous
and the country often so rough and ruggedly stark that one can not
reasonably take chances.

In some of the remote mountains where we've camped, our
planned destination has been in view and yet more than a week
away if we'd attempted walking directly to it. The important question in such circumstances becomes less one of where our objective
is than one of how to reach there.

Ordinarily, though, finding your way about can be so easy that
it barely needs much planning—with one vital exception. In the
event of an unexpected storm or abruptly blanketing weather, you
should always be ready to get to where you are going by compass.

Otherwise, let's presume that two miles due west of your campfire there is a height topped by a peculiarly outlined mesa. This
distinctive eminence you can see for miles, watching its outline
changing as you travel. By keeping track of this mesa, you can
gauge almost exactly where your camp lies in relation to it. If you
continue glancing back and considering the look of things, you'll
be easily able to return over your outward route.

Getting There and Back on Your Own

Nobody is going to feel really confident, relaxed, and com-
fortably contented where the sands stretch to the horizion until he
understands the simple principles of finding his way anywhere and,
alone or not, of always knowing for sure where he is.

The feat of keeping found is not as perplexing as it may first
appear. Anywhere on land, certainly, you can keep a record of your

comings and goings with a map, a compass, and some means of marking it down. Every dozen minutes and every occasion you head in another direction is the time, at least initially, to bring that map up to the present moment.

Not everyone will have a map of the area. Then using the range, road, or region from which you started as the beginning point, just sketch your own map as you go along. An acquaintance scratched one on his binoculars.

The most weather-rusted desert rat uses exactly the same technique, whether aware of it or not. His map is in his head, that's all. Sun, moon, stars, vegetation, slant, and any number of other natural factors may be his compass—so long as, it should be thoroughly realized, conditions remain favorable.

Watching the Distance

A watch is of some especial value when traveling the desert afoot, not only because you can determine direction with its help, but also because it affords the most practical method of measuring how far you go.

Whether the hour and minute the timepiece indicates is accurate or otherwise is not the critical factor when you're concerned with how much ground you cover rather than whatever the Greenwich time may be. Any watch running at a constant speed will do, although if, aside from distance, you wish to be in closer ratio with the standard or daylight time, you can so set the watch with the help of the sun and its shadow.

One absorbs the truth early in unfamiliar regions that where you go upon leaving camp for the day may be across flat and open country. Or, curious, you may follow a game trail that winds the same number of miles up hills and down through twisting canyons. If one is unaccustomed to desert travel, a rule of thumb is to multiply your estimates of distance by three, as both the clear, dry air and the frequent absence of land features tend to make underestimation likely.

Suppose that on the way back you encounter a congenial and gray-whiskered prospector, still on his lifetime quest for gold, at the junction of two trails each of which roughly heads in the direction of the mesa in whose shadow you've pitched your tent. It's only logical to inquire how far it is along each trail to where you want to reach.

His laconic answer, "Both are five miles," still leaves you undecided, as he figured it would.

If he replies instead, "The left trail is an easy two hours. I suppose you could get there along the right-hand path by sundown if you rustled right along," you'll know just about what to expect.

The Wheel Spokes Some Call Degrees

A circle is a circle. No matter what its area, each will divide into 360 equally separated degrees. So it is with compass dials, where straight lines from the center to the rim may perhaps be most easily visualized as 360 possible routes, fanning out like wheel spokes from wherever you happen to be.

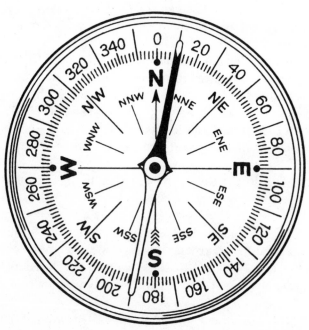

You will feel more confident, relaxed, and comfortable about travelling in the desert if you carry a compass and know how to use it.

Compass degrees are customarily numbered in a clockwise direction, starting at north. East is one-fourth of the way around the dial. East in terms of degrees is, therefore, one-fourth of 360° or 90°.

The distance between each of the four cardinal points—north, east, south, and west—is the same 90°. South is often designated as 180° and west as 270°.

Northeast is halfway between north and east. Northeast in terms of degrees is, then, half of 90° or 45°. Half of that again is 22.5°, which is north-northeast.

Declination by Night

The actuality that the entire earth is a magnet can complicate compass reading. In the Sun Belt's deserts, the result is that compasses are diverted eastward. The culprit is the magnetic north. This is ever shifting some fourteen hundred miles south and east of the geographic North Pole, off Canada's polar coast.

This declination, marked on many maps, is necessary to know if you are traveling by printed map or by natural signs influenced by the sun. The better commercial maps indicate it. It is not necessary, however, to consult such a map to learn the compass declination in your area.

It's easy enough to find the compass declination on a clear night by seeing for yourself how closely your compass points toward the North Star. If your compass does not have a luminous dial, mark the direction from where you are to the North Star with a scratched line or a straight stick. Then in the morning make your comparison. The difference between where the North Star is located and where your compass points will be the local declination.

Although generally your compass will point toward the magnetic north, nearby influences can throw it off. The most diverting factor can be natural ore deposits, sometimes not a bad thing to know. Others may be guns, flashlights, metal fishing rods, battery-powered watches, the photoelectric cells in exposure meters and some cameras, and the like. For accurate bearings, it's sound practice to consult your compass as far from such distractions as you are knowingly able to get.

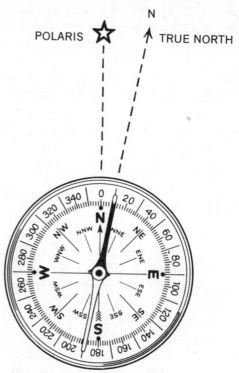

It's easy to find the compass declination on a clear night. Mark the direction from where you are to the North Star with a scratched line or a straight stick. Then in the morning, compare the difference between where the North Star is located and where your compass points. That is the local declination.

The Compass of Professionals

The professionals' compass—relied upon by explorers, surveyors, engineers, geologists, timber cruisers, and the serious orienteers whose choice often is a Silva—is based on a counterclockwise system of numbering. North is still 0°. The other degrees and points are read around to the left.

By far the finest I've come by is a magnificent British surveyors' compass of circa 1850–1880, with a clinometer for determining angles of elevation or inclination. Made by F. Barner and Son of London for E. Esdaile Sidney, it was given to me when we were b'iling the kittle on a memorable afternoon by a close personal friend, James F. M. Day, who for thirty years was managing editor of one of the world's great newpapers.

Also a licensed navigator, among other achievements, Jim Day used one like it when a youth with the Coast Geodetic Survey in Alaska where, keeping the camp in meat in his spare time, he started his record book with a trophy brown bear.

"Such an instrument provides that it may be set for local variation (indicated on every proper map)," Mr. Day said, "and then with its dial graduated in 360 degrees running counterclockwise, and the east and west letters on the face plate reversed, every bearing is a true bearing conforming to the geographic north and not the magnetic north.

"All the formerly bewildered voyageur has to do is point the sighting device on the compass at his landmark and read the true bearing *off the north end of the needle!*

"Conversely, in setting a course, the woodsman orients the pointers or sights of his pocket transit and then reads the true geographic course off the north end of the needle. For instance, if he wants to go straight east, he swings the north end of the needle to *E*, or 90°, and the sights on the compass will indicate a true east bearing.

"If he should wish to go due south, he turns the compass till the north end of the needle is at the *S* mark, or 180°, looks along the sights, and he is headed toward Antarctica. To go west he would move the north end of the needle to 270°.

"In making these tentative operations in using an engineer's compass, it will readily be seen why the east and west letters are always reversed on a pocket transit or Brunton. Also why the 360° scale runs counterclockwise.

"It is the simplest and best type of compass to use once the trick is mastered," Jim Day told me. "Additionally, this type of compass is traditionally equipped with a level and a clinometer for measuring vertical angles and percentages of gradient."

Compass Attachment

For everyday wanderings never far from the sound of civilization, where pinpoint precision is unnecessary, the small, rugged, waterproof, luminous Marble's Pin-on Compass can be handy. Fastened to the outside of clothing at breast-pocket level, it is constantly where it can be glanced at for quick checks without even stopping. The fact that the entire dial moves makes such checks still easier.

If you like this sort of arrangement, there's also now the similarly luminous and lightweight Williams Guide Line Compass, giving you a choice. The Williams instrument sticks out further, based as it is on a floating sphere. On the other hand, it freely revolves at all angles and generally keeps itself even more level. How tough its plastic is in comparison to Marble's certainly sturdy metal, we haven't taken a rock and tested.

The Compass You Can Make

You can even make a momentary compass if you happen to have, along with some water, a small, slim length of steel such as a sewing needle.

Stroke the metal in a single direction for a minute or two with a magnet or a piece of silk. Then rub the now-magnetized metal between your forefinger and thumb after getting these extremities a bit oily by rubbing them over your nose.

Locate some quiet water next, maybe a bright little pool cupped in a boulder, or just a nonmetallic dish partially filled for the time being from your canteen. Take two threads, two thin lengths of grass, or such. Double these to make two loops in which you cradle the needle. Lower the latter's lean length carefully to the water's surface.

You'll see the top of the fluid bending under the needle's weight, if all goes well, as the surface tension keeps it afloat. The now unrestrained needle, responding to this hemisphere's magnetic north, will slowly turn until it extends a dozen degrees or so south and east of the North Pole.

If you have stroked the needle from eye to tip, the eye will point northward.

From Watch to Compass

A watch used as a makeshift compass in the United States and Canada can be relied upon to be true within 8 degrees, depending upon where you happen to be in any of the 15-degree-wide time zones.

Three factors are prerequisites: The sun must be shining brightly enough to throw a shadow, the timepiece must be accurately set, and it must show the local standard Greenwich time.

Then it's a matter of laying the watch face up with the hour hand pointing directly toward the sun. This position we can check by holding a straight twig or stem upright at the edge of the dial and turning the dial if necessary until its shadow lies directly along the watch's hour hand.

South will then lie midway along the smaller arc between the hour hand and 12 o'clock. If such a procedure is carried out at 9:00 A.M. standard time, a line drawn from the center of the watch outward through the 10:30 position will point south.

The Compass-Regulated Watch

By reversing this principle you can ascertain Greenwich time by employing a compass.

It is then the compass which must be accurate when you are using it to determine hours. Therefore, the local magnetic decli-

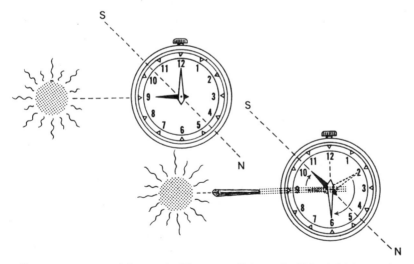

You can use your watch for a makeshift compass if the sun is shining brightly enough to throw a shadow and the timepiece is accurately set for local standard Greenwich time.

nation must be reckoned with. If you do not already know it, the North Star can inform you (see "Declination by Night" earlier in this chapter).

The compass is used to determine due south. Then with the help of a shadow to keep the watch's hour hand pointing toward the sun, turn this hand until south is centered in the shorter arc between it and the numeral 12. This will set the watch to within a few minutes of the local standard time.

Mapped Importance

There can be difficulty in traveling intelligently without a map for any substantial distance in some parts of unknown and unmarked wilderness. It is only reasonable foresightedness, therefore, to study beforehand whenever possible whatever maps there may be, however sketchy, of the region through which you're journeying.

Besides being sound procedure in case you suddenly find yourself off track and on your own, such a practice enhances anyone's anticipation and enjoyment of the drive, cruise, backpacking trip, or whatever.

Knowing what you're flying over, too, can make any flight more interesting, while even cursory knowledge of this sort could ward off needless difficulties in the event of a forced landing, especially in the mountains.

Where They Are

For maps of any area in the United States, write for the free Topographic Map Index Circular of the state in which your interest lies and for the publication *Topographic Maps*. A postcard to the U. S. Geological Survey, Map Information Office, Arlington, Virginia 22202 will do.

The Index, which notes prices, shows a map of the entire area divided into quadrangles. Identify the quadrangle in which you are interested and mail your request to the U. S. Geological Survey, Federal Building, Denver, Colorado 80225. Include a check, or to save perhaps a couple of weeks, a money order. This office also handles serial photographs, togographic maps, and geodetic survey controls for each state, Puerto Rico, the Virgin Islands, American Samoa, and Guam. Most desirable may be the contour maps available.

For regions not on regular topographical maps, and for information concerning maps produced by government agencies, a good source is the National Cartographic Information Center, U.S. Geological Survey, 507 National Center, Reston, Virginia 22092.

Price lists covering maps of all units of the National Park Service are sent from the Office of Information, National Park Service, Eighteenth and C Streets NW, Washington, DC 20249.

Nearly three million maps and charts, thirty thousand atlases, several hundred globes and models, and a fifty-card bibliography of cartographical literature are to be found in the Map Reading Room, Library of Congress, First Street and Independence Avenue SE, Washington, DC 20540.

Data on the ordering of both free and priced maps and other publications appear in the *Library of Congress Publications in Print,* revised annually and available free from the Office of the Secretary of the Library at the same address.

Write for pamphlet FS-13 to the Forest Service, U.S. Department of Agriculture, Washington, DC 20259 for the addresses of the ten regional offices of the National Forest Ranger Districts, as well as other sources from which often free maps, strong on access roads and other man-made features, can be secured.

For government maps of nearby Mexico, a source to which to address your inquiries is the Direccion de Geografia y Meteorologia, Tacusaya, D. F., Mexico.

Private sources of both domestic and foreign maps include: The National Geographic Society, Seventeenth and M Street NW, Washington, DC 20036, and the International Map Company, 595 Broad Avenue, Ridgefield, NJ 07657. The society's scope is well known, of course, while the latter company has a large stock of United States and Canadian topographic maps as well as those of other countries.

For air photos, which in many instances should be ordered at least half a year in advance, write for the free *Status of Aerial Photography* to the Map Information Office, U. S. Geological Survey, Washington, DC 20242. This publication indicates the availability and source of the government agency or private company holding the desired negative from which the order can be printed, all of which takes correspondence, identification, and time.

Saving Time with the Contours

Contour maps are far and away the most invaluable in Sun Belt country still scarcely touched by human feet, indicating as they do the mesas, buttes, valleys, mountains, and twining canyons in terms of elevations. Consulting such a chart even on the desert-rimming ridges can eliminate a parching amount of wasted climbing, descending, and then scaling again.

Even when traveling by compass in a straight line is possible, it's often no more advisable than might be expected. In the heights coolly rearing from sun-scorched sand, one soon confirms that both thirsty time and strength can be conserved by circling several miles along a ridge, instead of striking a small fraction of that distance straight across a tantalizingly narrow ravine to the same destination.

Common Sense

The main safeguard when back of beyond and on the move is either to be sure of the basic topographical facts or not to depend on them. Skid, tote, and other roads come to dead ends. Prominent ridges melt into level country. Even large streams disappear underground, sometimes for miles at a time.

Before entering sheer wilderness anywhere it can be a profitable practice, even when you have what seems to be a reliable map, to have some old-timer update, supplement, and perhaps correct it, particularly if you're in one of the rougher regions where even the most diligent and ambitious surveying crew can do only a sketchy job in the time allotted. Aerial mapping in many such sections has turned out vastly improved maps, but country looks different when one is afoot.

No matter where you got your map, either be as absolutely certain as possible of the accuracy of its basic topographical details, or do not ever rely on them. The road you were planning to intercept after the day's activities may have come to an abrupt end shortly after you left it. A high ridge you've been using as a landmark for miles may, ahead, dwindle into levelness. Even large streams have sometimes vanished underground, occasionally for miles, where you've been depending on reaching them.

Translating What's There

The thing to do initially when you spread out your map at some vantage point in unfamiliar country is of course to orient it. With most, true north is at the top. When it isn't, the map is usually so marked. Very often the magnetic north, where your compass will point in that particular region, is also indicated.

When your map is turned so that its north is in line with actual north, it will show the direction from where you are presently located to the major features of the landscape it depicts. From where you are, for instance, a butte appears on the map some three miles away, as measured by its scale, in a southeasterly direction. If you travel southeast for roughly three miles, you'll be at the butte.

Say you're at the butte with some of the fossils you'd been seeking already pocketed, and the map shows the junction of the two canyons where your tent is pitched. Orient your map again, lay a straw on it between where you are and where you want to reach, and pointing directly toward your camp will be the telltale straw.

Which Watershed?

In big country it is the broad watersheds that keep you better oriented, rather than the rivers and rills or the ruts they have engraved as their part of this planet's autobiography. This takes a lot of attention, though. In areas such as some near the Continental Divide, only a few feet separate waters that on the west may flow into the Pacific and on the east eventually reach the Atlantic.

This happened to one of us during an autumn when an elk was needed for food, and the situation could have been critical if a compass hadn't been also in use. We'd pitched our tent by a river and, having no set destination any day, settled into the practice of following some stream down out of the mountains late afternoons until reaching a recognizable part of the river.

What happened on this particular day, the reconstructed facts revealed, was that a saddle so low it was not perceived became unknowingly crossed. But on the way down a brook that afternoon, it soon became evident something was amiss. That water ended up in another stream fifty miles from the destination desired. Upon rerouting the way by compass, it became apparent that this particular saddle, insignificant though it was in those high mountains, marked the division of the local watersheds.

The Exits of Experience

If camp lies against some very long and easily followed land-mark, such as the base of a prominent ridge, getting back after a day afield can be practically foolproof. Anyone experienced in desert travel so situates his camp whenever possible, for he will still be able to find it although the weather becomes stormy and the night black.

Say the lengthy ridge extends north and south. Presume that when you head away from it, you go east. Then any time you continue traveling west while on your way back, you are bound to reach the foot of the elevation.

If you happen to be camped instead on the west side, it's merely a matter of reversing the direction and heading east. After even rough general reckoning, you will be halted by the ridge along whose bottom you're camped.

The Logic of Bearing to One Side

The preceding is admittedly a broad example, for all of us will normally want to keep sufficient track of our whereabouts to be able to intersect such a broadside within a reasonable distance of the spot desired. The question of which way to turn, too, ordinarily should not be left to chance.

Coming upon an unmarked destination directly involves such a disproportionate percentage of chance that rarely is it wise even to attempt to pinpoint your return. Unless there are guiding factors such as landmarks on which you can rely, the more expert technique is to bear definitely to one particular side of the target. Then upon reaching the lateral, you will immediately know in which direction to follow it.

The Plus that Orienteering Offers

A relatively new sport in the United States that was imported from Scandinavia is the orienteering mentioned earlier. It is dry land navigation basically, with the aid of a compass and a topographic map. Individuals or teams start from a chosen point and, using the map and compass, attempt to navigate from point to point in the shortest time possible.

The competitor may be given the full details of an entire route at the onset, or he may have to get separate instructions about reaching the next checkpoint or "control" as he goes along. Sometimes he must follow a prescribed path between controls. Other forms of the sport permit the competitor to choose his own route between points and in some cases even the order in which the checkpoints are approached. Usually, though, the course returns to its starting point for the finish.

Different categories of skill permit beginners to compete against beginners and the experts to fight it out among themselves. There are a lot of variations in scoring. In general, the game involves reading a map accurately and, with the help of your compass, relating this information to the actual land in front of you, physically finding specific places as rapidly as possible.

Often, it is better to read the map and follow roads, or at least avoid any cliffs or bogs or rivers, than simply to aim straight for the next checkpoint no matter what the terrain may be.

That is the whole challenging skill of this sport: to read the map, to interpret it in terms of what you yourself see, to reach the most reasonable conclusion as to how to get where you're going first, and then use your compass to bring it off.

Orienteering has been practiced by Boy Scouts and Marines, by youngsters and oldsters, and by highly competitive and by equally noncompetitive individuals everywhere. Sometimes it turns up, as it did during the boyhood of one of us, in the appealing guise of treasure hunting.

It goes on all over the country. Look around, if it seems appealing, for it may already be in your area. At least it is an enjoyable way to spend a healthy day in the out-of-doors. Besides all the fun, it can be a sugar-coated opportunity for practicing some very practical survival skills that later could make the difference in less ideal circumstances, as when one is lost and suddenly orienteering becomes no longer a game.

The Polestar

No sign in this hemisphere affords a more reliable means for pinpointing north when the North Star is visible than this orb, also known as Polaris. The bright polestar seems to the naked eye to be pretty much alone in the heavens. Ordinarily it is most readily located by following an imaginary line up through the two stars that mark the outer edge of the Big Dipper.

Polaris is such an infallible signpost that if we are close to anyone who does not already know its whereabouts well, we may want to show that individual with the least reasonable delay how to be able always to recognize it. Not only can such knowledge be of help on inestimable occasions when there may a doubt about direction, but times innumerable it has saved lives, and the next life so involved may be one more important to you than your own.

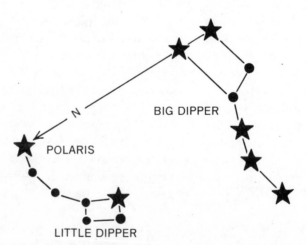

Polaris, or the North Star, is nature's reliable means for pinpointing north. In the Northern Hemisphere, the North Star is never more than roughly one degree from the celestial North Pole or true north. Ordinarily the North Star can be located by following an imaginary line up through the two stars that mark the outer edge of the Big Dipper.

W or Is It M?

Most are aware that, depending on when we look at them, the five stars known as Cassiopeia appear either as an *M* or a *W*. This northern constellation is always on the opposite side of the North Star from the Big Dipper and about the same distance away.

By memorizing the relationship between Cassiopeia and Polaris, we can use the former for finding north when the Big Dipper is invisible.

Direction by Any Star

With the way the earth continually revolves, stars seem to swing from east to west in great arcs, forming the white streaks that puzzle those first looking at time-exposure pictures of the night sky. The way in which any star seems to move can furnish us, therefore, with a general idea of direction.

We have to take a sight, first of all, for the movement is too gradual to detect just by glancing at the heavens. We will need two fixed points over which to watch, and these may be the sights of a stationary rifle, or two stakes driven into the ground for the purpose with their tops lined up carefully. If we will observe a star over them for several minutes, it will seem to rise, to move to one side or the other, or to sink.

If the star we are observing seems to be lifting in the heavens, we are looking approximately east; if it appears to be falling, it is situated generally west of us. If the star has the appearance of looping flatly toward our right, we are facing roughly south. If it gives the impression of swinging rather flatly toward our left, then we are heading just about north.

All this is more evident in the profound clear dark where the stars no longer shiver in half-luminescent haze and, in chill desert solitudes, their glimmer crusts into frozen glitter.

6

Safety Is No Accident

Once one realizes even subconsciously that circumstances are such that he can not afford to have an accident, probabilities shift markedly against any mishap happening. Nowhere is this more apparent than out in the desert.

The reason is that what may be but a self-punishing, or attention-getting, or a responsibility-relieving misstep where help is at hand, can be extremely serious when you are days from anyone else, even when the going is at its best.

The only reasonable rule in remote, sandy regions is never to take an unnecessary chance, weighing always the possible loss against the potential gain, and going about life with as wide a safety margin as practical.

Away from the masses, too, one is not so apt to become entangled in the lapses and shortcomings of others.

---

opposite page: Almost everybody who spends time in the desert sooner or later chances into a prickly cactus. For protection, wear loose clothing that covers the body while you are wandering in cactus territory, like the man walking between the two organ pipe cacti in this photograph.

"Nothing is so much to be feared as fear," Thoreau noted early. But he added, "A live dog is preferable to a dead lion."

What's Surest When You're Unsure

When we lack the personal experience that would enable us to make our own credible evaluation of a situation, it is natural to accept the combined opinions of others. The unfortunate thing about this is that many widely popular beliefs are definite and positive in reverse ratio to their lack of foundation in fact.

When long accepted but nevertheless wholly false tenets increase in assurance the oftener they are repeated, this many times in highly respected published sources, they can not help but become more dangerous.

When unsure of the best or even the preferable procedure in an emergency, the likelihood is that you'll do better to let common sense be the determining factor rather than some not-altogether-logical method about which you may have heard.

It was not until well within this century that Vilhjalmur Stefansson noted the British officially began taking steps to prevent scurvy in their crews in the way that actually works.

Flash Floods

A sudden wall of water and then the following torrent—sweeping down the parched courses of streams, creeks, culverts, ditches, and river bottoms, and, in a flood, across low-lying land—is the desert's most dangerous drama.

These can happen, where they do, whenever heavy rain or rapidly melting snow fill the eroded and the constructed drainage systems to overflowing. Mainly they appear in the mountainous areas. The sometimes almost unbelievable savagery of a flash flood may move for miles, however, over relatively flat terrain, collecting debris and mud which increase the destruction they can bring to everything in their way.

The warning can be the faraway buildup of heavy, dark clouds, silhouetted at night by lightning flashes, all indicative of potential nearing thunderstorm activity. The National Weather Service broadcasts alerts and continuing information about surface conditions and weather.

The various governments' flash flood safety rules envelop the general situation:

1. Do not camp or park in dry stream beds or washes.
2. When planning a trip into areas where flash floods are possible, inform someone of your itinerary and expected time of return. Stick with your plan, and check in when you return.
3. Carry a portable radio or use the car radio to keep alert to weather conditions.
4. Never cross a water-filled highway dip until making sure of water depth and road condition. The roadway may be washed out.
5. If your car is damaged or stalled, stay near it on high ground. Search and rescue parties will locate a vehicle much more quickly than a person.

Thirst-Quencher of the Desert

When the Spanish conquistadores early explored the New World's Southwest, they found the natives eating the tiny little white, brown, and gray seeds of the *Salvia,* or chia. A single teaspoonful of the seeds of this mint family member was deemed enough to sustain an Indian for a day on a forced march.

When added to a cup of water and soaked for several minutes, a similar amount of chia seeds provides in the desert's dry heat an almost tasteless, yet unusually refreshing beverage, not only for satisfying thirst but also for offsetting the harshness of alkaline springs.

The easiest way to gather chia is to take some sort of a receptacle in one hand and a stick in the other, then knock the seeds into the container by striking the dry flower tops. All a starving man has to do to get part of all the vitamins, minerals, and other nutriments is to eat a pinch of the seeds dry, or soak them to drink. Soaking them will cause each seed to become separately suspended in its own whitish mucilaginous coat.

The highly digestible gruel made by mixing such chia with water is eaten still in Mexico's hinterlands and, further diluted,

Chia, Salvia

Chia or *Salvia* is known as the thirst-quencher of the desert. A single teaspoonful of the seeds was enough to sustain an Indian for a day on a forced march.

served instead of water in lead-crystal glasses clinking with ice in some of its cities' swankiest restaurants and chic sidewalk cafes.

Chia continues to be highly regarded medically in some circles. For instance, several seeds placed under the eyelids when you go to bed will help clear the eyes of minor inflammation. A paste made by soaking a few seeds in a little water is used both as a salve for inflamed membranes and a poultice for gunshot wounds.

A dose made by stirring a teaspoonful of the seeds in a glass of cold water, then letting the mixture stand for several minutes, can settle a disturbed stomach and nourish you at the same time.

Chance Encounters with Cactus

Almost everybody chances into one of our prickly neighbors sooner or later. Some cacti have regular daggers they drive deep into the tissues of any encounterer. Others protect themselves with hairlike projections that cause itching and redness and are close to impossible to remove. Some have the capacity to set up an intense inflammatory response. In any case, they tend to hang on once they have made contact, and there is no handle to pull them loose.

For this reason, but more for its insulating qualities, loose clothing that covers the body is best while you are wandering in cactus territory. Solid boots are less likely to be penetrated by thorns than are the cooler slippers. Prevention is once again a good idea. Avoidance is even better.

If a burr or loose segment of cactus does stick to you, you'll find a coarse-toothed comb a handy tool for removing the part that has attached itself. Just slide the teeth beneath it and flick outward. It works on horses and dogs.

For the ones with hairlike thorns, such as the Teddy Bear cholla, many of the little needles may be left in the skin and will work their way inward, causing pain, swelling, and possibly infection. If they still project beyond the skin, an application of collodion over them will sometimes harden into a coat that can be peeled off, taking the offending hairs with it. Ask your druggist about collodion and its substitutes.

For the larger needles, it is well to try to remove them as promptly as possible. Motion will cause them to break off or work their way deeper into the tissues, and removing them can become a minor surgical procedure. For the extraction, tweezers are useful. So is a small magnifying glass on occasion, and it can be used to light campfires also.

A Course in First Care

A myriad of mishaps not peculiar to the desert can happen there as well as anywhere. Things like falls, broken bones, concussions, and serious cuts are possible in the back country as well as in the backyard.

A good first aid course including emergency cardiopulmonary resuscitation (CPR) might well be the most effective and least expensive source of information about first care you'll ever encounter. Back of beyond it could, some unexpected time, well make the difference in what can be the most unforgiving climate in the world.

The Safety Margin

When we are coming down an eroded bank or, in fact, any downgrade, there is a basic safety principle which we all recognize but sometimes overlook in the exhilaration of a descent. It is so to control our center of gravity that if we do fall, it will be backward in maneuverable sliding position.

Such a precaution, we come more and more to realize, is of the utmost importance during solitary travel over new paths, where rotten rock common in desert country has not before been disturbed by man and where decomposing vegetation has not been tried.

The identical principle holds even when we are traveling among obstructions on a flat, for it is a sometimes too costly convenience to let the body drop or swing forward to rest a hand momentarily on a projection and vault ahead. The untested support to which we will then be committed may twist, roll, slide, or give away entirely.

Even though this may happen only one time in ten thousand in such a way that you will not be able to save yourself, unless there are extenuating circumstances the odds will be too far out of proportion with the possible gain to warrant taking such a gamble.

A reasonable precautionary attitude back of beyond is to expect to fall at any moment, for so realizing the possibility, we will be more likely to be prepared for it—by avoidance of an area; by extreme care when to bypass is not practical; and most commonly by continually gauging beforehand where and in what manner, if we do fall, we will be able to let ourselves go most safely.

The Desert's Indian Figs

The fruit of all the cacti can satisfactorily take the edge off your hunger. In the deserts and dry country there is the prickly pear or Indian fig, particularly relished once the spines are singed off in the campfire and the thin skins peeled off.

These are the little spiny knobs, ranging from the size of apricots to that of lemons, that bulge from the padlike joints of cactus.

This fruit of the opuntia cactus is easy to identify, but more difficult to pick. It's best to go at this ritual cautiously as you can with a knife and any other protection you can find.

Depending on the kind of cactus, the colors of ripened prickly pears vary from tawny green and purplish black to the choicest of them all, the big red fruits of the large *Opuntia megacantha* of the Southwest. To eat them, slice off the ends, slit the hide lengthwise, and scoop out the pulp.

Who Sometimes Rattle

The most common of the potentially serious snakebites are those of one of the twelve to eighteen varieties of rattlesnakes found in our western deserts.

Such bites are frequently caused when inebriated rattlesnake owners, fascinated by these pit vipers, are playing with them. The first lesson, then, would be: don't play with rattlesnakes.

Though it has been said that you can not walk a mile in the desert without passing within ten feet of a rattler, it is rare to see one unless you spend a lot of time hunting doves in the maize and cotton fields around the big cities.

Watch where you put your hands and feet. If you do see a rattlesnake, leave it alone! Generally, it will reciprocate and leave you alone, too. There are perhaps fifty to a hundred bites each year in Arizona alone but fatalities are not common. Rattlesnakes have the ability to inject or withhold their venom, and it has been estimated that only 60 to 80 percent of the humans they do bite have received venom. Then it is a question of the type of snake, the size of any dose of venom, the part of the body struck, and the health of the victim.

Debate vigorously continues about the proper first care and definitive care of rattlesnake bites. Here is a personal medical opinion.

The first thing you need to know is if you have been envenomated. Generally, increasing local pain and swelling, along with a tingling around the mouth, signal the presence of venom. These symptoms take about five to fifteen minutes to surface. During that interval, the best opportunity to cut and suck, or to excise (which is to cut the bite out), will be slipping away.

In most untrained hands, cutting large crosses into unanesthe-tized portions of anatomy is probably as dangerous as the snakebite. Carving out a chunk of the local topography is even worse.

If your bite occurs in the entryway to the emergency department of your local hospital, that type of procedure may be in order. At the other extreme, if definitive care is several days away and you feel competent to undertake the cut and suck, then it may be in order.

In general, I think it better not to go ahead with it if there is a reasonable chance of reaching help. It is because to the inexpe-rienced person, personally involved, the damage from any such snakebite usually appears worse than the eventual outcome. Con-servatism in treatment gives good results.

Incidentally, almost any snake has bacteria in its mouth, so there is the possibility of secondary infections. Nonpoisonous snakes bite, too, if pushed to it.

Then there is the frequently advised nonconstricting tourniquet, with its sound of a contradiction in terms. If you can pass several fingers under a loop placed around an extremity, what is it impeding? Only if and when the limb actually swells to tighten the tourniquet will it accomplish anything, and that, interfering with the blood supply, may be the wrong thing. It all has the semblance of a gesture and not much more. Some experts support its use, however.

What about keeping the limb dependent—that is, lower than the heart? It is probably wise to keep the venom lower than the heart. But if the circulation is working, and it must to pump blood to your head, what you hope to do is slow entry *into* the circulation. That depends on the blood supply of the part struck and whether a larger vessel was entered. Most fangs are limited in penetration to less than an inch, so it is the skin and subcutaneous fat that gets any poison. Exceptions are the hands or the feet, and, as with cactus thorns, loose clothing can help here.

Dependency will probably cause greater swelling, as will im-mobility. Keeping the struck limb level, but below heart level, is probably best. About 98 percent of the bites are on the arms or the legs, usually the legs, except among the bibulous snake-handlers who get them on the arms.

There was at one time a strong sentiment for immersing snake-bites in cold water. Local cooling will constrict the skin's blood in the area, but prolonged wetting probably will macerate the tissues more than anything. Dry cooling, if you have it, might help. Some feel it potentiates the poison.

Finally, what about carrying antivenom? Injecting this horse serum product can cause serum sickness; in fact, it is *expected* to cause serum sickness. So you have to be prepared to desensitize those who are sensitive to horse serum, and then treat the serum sickness after giving an adequate dose of this polyvalent antidote.

The material outdates, so that no doubt Murphy's Law would function and all of your antivenom will be too old. It takes anywhere from four to thirty vials given intravenously to accomplish the desired neutralization, and that is rather a lot to carry around. Injecting the material around the bite has received mixed reviews. It isn't clear that it works very well. In short, injecting one vial of antivenom subcutaneously or intramuscularly when in the field is probably not wise.

So, what are we left with as reasonable treatment for a rattlesnake bite in most circumstances? Try to see what kind of a rattler it was—the type if possible and whether it was large or small. Be calm and assess your location, where you were bitten, and whether or not you seem to have received venom. If definitive care can be reached without overly stressing yourself, then do so without undue haste.

If not, consider the cut-and-suck, a tourniquet, and rest. Recovery can take quite a while, so that in a survival situation, a snakebite can be bad news indeed. If you have water, weighing one thing against another, it may be best to send for, or wait for, help.

It is assumed that one has not been so short sighted as to go out into the desert without telling anyone where he or she is going and when to expect one's return. This applies to camping, backpacking, airplane flights, or an afternoon in the Chiracahuas; make a plan, communicate it, and stick to it.

The Beaded Lizard and Some Others

There are, of course, snakes and poisonous creatures other than rattlers. The coral snake abides in the Sonoran Desert and in Florida. These little creatures have a poison related to cobra venom. They are very small, fortunately, and their bites are very rare. Since there is not much else to do, they should be treated as rattlesnake bites are. There is an antivenom for Florida coral snakes, but not for those in the Sun Belt of the Southwest (in actuality far, far more timid than troublesome).

Then there is the Gila monster and, about the border and in the north of Mexico, the Mexican beaded lizard. Once again, they have a very potent toxin. The delivery system, however, is not very good, and you would have to go out of your way to get bitten. The message here is, once again, leave them alone, and they will leave you alone. One of us had a Gila monster as a neighbor for some months, but eventually the goings and comings may have become too busy for him and he moved out.

Spiders and Such

One of the most villainous-appearing arachnids in the world is the tarantula. They are big, hairy, and, in the desert, very common, dwelling in holes in the ground. They are relatively harmless although they can bite. A child could get sick from the bite, but barring some other disease they don't cause much harm and rather than being dangerous, are interesting to watch.

The Arizona brown spiders are different. These *Loxosceles*, related to the Brown Recluse of the Midwest, can cause pain along with loss of tissue at the site of a bite. The wound is characteristic, but it takes a little time to develop. There is a central blanching surrounded by a swollen red areola, which is very sore. The central area dies, becomes blue-black, and finally sloughs out, leaving a secondary wound to heal in.

Initial care is rather limited: cleansing, splinting, elevation, and rest. Definitive care is limited also, since it seems nearly impossible to halt the tissue death in the center of the wound.

Black widow spiders occur in the desert also. Where both sexes of the brown spiders can cause envenomation, it is the female who is the problem here. The male has venom but is too small to penetrate most people's skin.

The bite itself may be a minor thing in contrast to that of the brown spider. The rigors associated with the systemic response, however, can be mistaken for an acute surgical abdomen, pain, fever, severe gastrointestinal upset, urgently indicating a need for medical attention to avoid unnecessary risks. If you know it is a black widow bite, there is an antivenom available. It is worth knowing, but it is not often necessary.

Again, first care is rather limited, being mainly supportive. Rest and avoidance of vigorous activities are generally sufficient. Diet should be liquids mainly, since gastrointestinal upsets are common. Generally, the major symptoms take from a quarter to a half an hour to develop, and pass off in several hours. One may be left with a generalized malaise for several days.

Both of these spiders like cracks, crannies, old buildings, and dimly lit places. They flourish in deserted old dwellings and can get into the back of your closet. The best defense is being aware that they are around, watching out for webs, and being careful to look before reaching.

Scorpions, Centipedes, and Millipedes

Let's differentiate between bites and stings. So far, the gist has been bites. The scorpion stings. It has a stinger on its tail and delivers its venom over its back. Most of them are not very serious, but the *Centuroides sculpturatus* of Sonora and Arizona can cause death in small victims and the elderly. There is an antivenom in Mexico for this little yellow devil.

It used to be commonplace to shake your clothes out and turn your boots upside down before dressing. One of us remembers, from not so very far back, a scorpion being so dislodged from a shirt left on the ground. He has also shaken centipedes out of his boots. Today in places where the population has expanded, such encounters are less and less likely. But it is possible for these crawling creatures to get into clothes baskets set upon the ground or to be brought in with fireplace wood. Certainly, if you are out in the desert, it is wise to look around before you sit on one.

Centipedes can bite. The bites can be painful, though ordinarily they are not serious. Millipedes can not bite, but they can excrete a noxious material if they are handled. The lesson: Don't handle them.

An acquaintance is allergic to the bite of the kissing bug, and even among those without such sensitivity, its bite can cause swelling and pain.

Then There's the Solpugids and Vinegaroons

Almost all arachnids and insects can bite or sting. Fire ants, lately becoming a spreading and serious problem in the South and Texas, can both bite *and* sting.

Most such bites and stings are not life-threatening unless there is a hypersensitivity reaction. Cooling, rest, perhaps a mild analgesic such as aspirin, cleansing of the bite, and an antihistamine are the essentials of any first aid.

Epinephrine subcutaneously is the specific for the so-called anaphylactic allergic response, resulting in shock, along with rapid transport to definitive medical care if that is possible. There are available kits that contain the appropriate materials that anyone with a known history of insect allergy should always carry.

Clearly, anyone with this kind of history takes a risk when out in the back country, but it should not be a prohibitive risk with planning and care. Knowing what can happen, and what to do if it does, is the most basic step in this area of possible risk in preparing for being abroad in the sandy spaces.

Besides, there are such as the vinegaroons, solpugids, and Jerusalem crickets! They are not only harmless, but are beneficial to mankind. Overall, as far as arachnids and insects are concerned, you're safer here than when getting here.

The Familiar and Most Often Fatal

The whole family of bees and wasps, hereabout and every-where, causes more deaths than all the snakes and scorpions to-gether. This is usually due to the potent allergic reactions that they can stimulate. Their various venoms are equally as potent as the snakes', but the dose is of course much smaller.

People who are sensitive to such as bee stings should have medical identification tags stating that information, have epinephrine always available, know how to inject themselves with it, and work hard at not getting stung.

Where Hypothermia Is More Than a Word

These deserts are cold lands on which the sun shines hot. At night, a campfire can become one's basic need. Here where, incongruously, hypothermia is not just a word, even an overnight hike in unfrequented stretches can be unwise for anyone without the means and knowledge to kindle a night blaze—one that will be warming until the sun takes over again.

The Whys Behind the Hows

Though campfires are made many ways, there is always the progression from spark to tinder to fuel. It is in these three essentials that the differences lie. An understanding of the fundamentals will add the sureness of logic to making, in any halfway-practical circumstance, that little blaze whose companionable warmth can mean life.

The first of these fundamentals is that it is not the firewood itself that burns. What does blaze is combustible gas. Enough heat has to produce enough gas from the fuel, this to combine with sufficient oxygen from the atmosphere to provide enough flame.

This, in turn, must itself be warm and long-lived enough to ignite the more and more gas it progressively produces from the continuing adequacy of the dead, dry pine twigs and sticks or other available fuel.

Bringing all this together in sleet or gale or other weather is more apt to be successful when it is approached knowledgeably and with thoughtful concern rather than haphazardly and helter-skelter— the way too many have tried to light their campfires.

The most practical way is with the familiar strike-anywhere wooden match. It follows that it is only sensible to keep a supply in a waterproof and unbreakable container whenever you are in the less- or never-traveled places. Even though at the time you may have a sufficient supply, it is still wisest to get in the habit of making that first match count. Such gradually acquired skill may one night mark the difference between a snug camp and one that's miserably damp and chilly.

The thing is to hold it so the fire can feed up the wood. This may mean facing a breeze with your hands cupped before the lighted match. You may kneel between the wind and your methodically piled wood so your body serves as a shield. You may use your spare shirt or any other convenient thing, perhaps a desiccated width of prickly pear, to guard the first wavering flames.

The Modest Metal Match

This ingenious invention will start a very great number of fires and remain intact despite most onslaughts of heat, cold, and moisture. One may be obtained inexpensively and should be a part of every basic outdoor kit. Just scrape a twinkling of the dark metal into the tinder, hold the stubby metallic stick against it, and strike it briskly with some such object as the back of your knife.

Then there are the lenses of cameras, binoculars, telescopes, and telescopic rifle sights that are excellent for pinpointing the sun for the production of fire. A little folding pocket magnifying lens will also turn the trick.

Securing necessary fuel can be more of a problem. This in some sandy regions is so rare that when you do locate suitable vegetation you'll find yourself utilizing all twigs, leaves, stems, and underground roots. Dry animal dungs can give a particularly hot flame whenever you venture where fuel is scarce; it is sound practice to gather a supply anytime this is possible.

The Invisible Enemy

Carbon monoxide can be a danger in any closed area where cooking or heating is being carried on with wood, alcohol, some oil products, or anything else containing carbon. The combination of carbon monoxide with the body's red blood corpuscles, which are thus prevented from replenishing themselves with oxygen in the air being breathed, can make this element deadly.

Just inhaling unsuspected small amounts of the odorless and invisible gas day after day can be fatal. The reason is that such otherwise inconsequential doses progressively join and remain in more and more hemoglobin until the next dose is the one too many.

The best precaution, as everywhere, is adequate ventilation. It would seem that a tent could therefore be one of the safest shelters. But when the spaces in the weave of ordinarily the most practical fabrics are closed by waterproofing in some instances and rain in others, little heaters and stoves have sometimes killed all occupants.

There's danger for newcomers who find out for themselves about winter in another world. Threatened are those few whose motor vehicles are held up when snow clogs that last high mountain pass. The tendency is to keep the windows tightly closed and the motor going to operate the heater. The peril, espeically if snow is drifting around the car, is in the carbon monoxide that can and too often does collect inside the unventilated vehicle.

In any situation there's seldom any hint of trouble, not even any breathing difficulty. Carbon monoxide usually gives no recognizable warning. What ordinarily occurs is that its victim is so abruptly overcome that by the time he realizes something is not right, he already is nearly if not completely helpless.

Carbon monoxide, like scurvy, has killed more individuals in North America from the equator to the Pole than will ever be known. Symptoms, if any are noticed, can start with headache, tightness over the forehead, and a slight flush. The headache becomes worse with continued exposure. Unless there's relief, dizziness, weakness, dimming vision, nausea, and vomiting can make their appearance.

With eventual collapse, the pulse and respiration quicken. Breathing may become alternately slower and labored. Coma comes, convulsions, slowing respiration and circulation, and finally nothing.

Fresh air can reverse all this if it is encountered soon enough. The response to unconsciousness is mouth-to-mouth resuscitation. This is better than the Shaefer and similar methods because of the 5 percent of carbon dioxide in the average rescuer's exhaled breath. The carbon monoxide in the system will dissipate faster if 5 to 10 percent carbon dioxide is supplied with the air that is forced into the lungs.

Carbon monoxide poisoning can be chronic. Continued exposure, as may happen when buildings are too tight or the exhaust systems of cars faulty, can cause chronic headaches, general sick feelings, digestive ailments, and the like, but never proceed further.

On desert roads, depending on the vehicle, there can be the choice between colder air conditioning and the bit more heat of windows slightly lowered, enough to let in a fraction more fresh air.

7

Being Your Own Desert Doctor

Author's Note: E. Russel Kodet, M.D., who is the coauthor of Being Your Own Wilderness Doctor *(Stackpole Books) kindly gave his valued and appreciated permission to use this material adapted from our still-current book.*

The skin stands between the rest of our body and the outside world. A skin burn is regarded as the worst injury that our reparative processes can face in terms of lost water, energy requirements, dangers of infection, and disability. Yet, the skin is constantly injured and continually repaired. Going out into the desert lays you open to a variety of problems.

A common response of the skin to injury of any kind is inflammation, with redness, swelling, pain, and frequent blistering as the signs. Allergies, toxic chemicals, infections, and injuries all show the common inflammatory pattern.

opposite page: Going out in the desert sun in an area like this one in Monument Valley, Arizona lays you open to a variety of problems, especially injuries to the skin.

Infections

Cellulitis is a bacterial infection of the skin from any break in its surface. The inflammation in this case is secondary to the bacterial presence in the skin and can follow any puncture, cut, abrasion, or burn.

If the skin is breached, as with an abrasion, the application of an antibiotic ointment or cream locally is the treatment of choice. It serves no purpose to smear a closed infection such as an abscess (boil) with ointments or drawing salves, since the antibiotic will not penetrate to the infection. For such infections, applications of warm, moist compresses for fifteen or twenty minutes, four to six times a day, help to localize the infection.

A more serious problem occurs when red streaks develop from a focus of infection up a limb. This is called lymphangitis and is often accompanied by chills and fever, systemic signs of infection. Place the part at rest, with a sling in the case of the hand or arm, or a crutch or bed rest in the case of the leg or foot. Try to elevate the infected part to improve circulation, so that the body can try to cure itself.

Start an oral antibiotic, and treat the affected area with warm, moist compresses as described above. Under ideal circumstances, they should be used continuously. Often, the streaking will disappear in twenty-four hours.

Often the lymph glands in the armpit or groin become swollen following an infection of that particular extremity. Antibiotics should be continued until the swelling and discomfort subside.

Boils and Other Abscesses

These usually come to a head, or the top surface softens. They are best opened when this occurs. It can be hastened with wet heat, as described.

Do not attempt to squeeze an abscess. Nature surrounds the abscess with a protective wall of white blood cells. Squeezing the boil breaks down this protective wall, and the germs are then forced into adjacent tissues. The infection then is no longer localized, but becomes a more serious diffused one. Open the boil with a single stab incision with the #11 Bard-Parker blade, as illustrated in Stackpole's *Being Your Own Wilderness Doctor*.

Danger Area—Face

There is a danger area on the face that deserves special mention. This area encompasses the upper lip, the nose, and the face immediately adjacent to the nose and beneath the eyes. Any infection in this region drains directly into the brain area without the protection of regional lymph glands. View all infection in this area as potentially serious and treat to the maximum. Above all, *never* squeeze an abscess in this area.

Intertrigo

This is a rash that occurs in warm, moist areas of the groin, the armpits, and other skin folds. Keeping the area dry and powdered with talc is the best prevention and treatment. Incidentally, the sometimes used boric acid *is a poison*. One is likely to get in trouble with it. The best thing is not to use it, for its merits are few and its complications many.

Dermatitis

Most typically, this is a weepy, moist area, resulting either from contact with poison oak and the like, or from any other substances to which the individual is allergic or sensitive.

Keep ointments off weepy areas. In general, cool, moist compresses are helpful. Witch hazel is ideal if it is available. Calamine lotion is the old standby, but in the bush relief from itching and irritation, as well as a specific therapeutic effect, can be had from starch baths or compresses. For large areas of the body, a starch bath will do miracles for itching and for soothing the area.

Stir a cup of starch into a quart of boiling water to make a colloidal suspension. This is now used for compresses, or it can be added to a tub of water for soaking large areas.

Cortisone ointments and creams are now available without a prescription. They are useful for this condition as well as for sunburn, poison ivy, and so on. They are applied locally or topically, as it is described, according to instructions on the tube.

Poison Ivy, Oak, and Sumac

Contact with these plants causes a skin irritation, first apparent as itchy bumps. Small blisters soon develop. The fluid in these is exceedingly irritating, so that scratching tends to spread the rash.

First, learn what these plants look like and avoid them. Be careful of the fumes of these growths when they are burning, as they can cause serious lung congestion. If you do come in contact with poison ivy, oak, or sumac, wash well with soap and water. Remove your clothing, and wash these before you wear them again.

Try at all costs to avoid scratching the affected areas. Pyribenzamine, 50 milligrams every four hours, is usually effective in helping the itch. So is aspirin, two 5-grain tablets every four hours. A paste of starch and water—or, better yet, starch boiled with a small amount of water to make a thick, gravylike concoction—can be applied locally to dry the blisters and to allay itching.

For large affected areas, if you have the facilities, make a starch bath by, first, adding a cup of starch such as flour to a quart of boiling water. This is stirred into a container of lukewarm water in 'which the patient soaks for fifteen to twenty minutes. The treatment is very soothing. An oatmeal bath can also be used, simply by substituting oatmeal for the starch.

When extreme cases do not respond to any of the above treatments, use the topical cortisone.

Hives

These pesky welts need no description. They itch and are uncomfortable, to say the least. They may be brought on by an insect bite, allergy to some food, or by a combination of factors such as fatigue and uneasy emotions. Treatment by use of laxatives and purgatives is not encouraged. Stay on an antihistamine Pyribenzamine, 50 milligrams every four hours, four times daily. The starch baths described before help. Cortisone also helps.

8

Humans and Heat

America's southwestern desert is coldly luring country where the sun overhead shines hot, and where any resulting problems can be solved advantageously, as you realize more and more the longer you live in this singular land of sun and sand.

A swimming pool can be numbingly cold when first you dive in on a searing day. The temperature becomes more tolerable after you have been in the water awhile, with the frequent sensation that somehow the pool is agreeably warming up. The hot day becomes cooler to you, although neither the water nor the temperature pressing upon it have actually changed at all—something which is often true with a lot of other things in life.

It was in Edward R. Frude's science class at Kimball Union Academy where one of us first heard about there being no such entity as cold, familiar though it seemed to be in the course of a

---

opposite page: If you find yourself stranded in the desert, you'll need to look for shelter and shade. The banks of valleys, dry rivers, and ravines are especially promising places to look for caves. Native American Indian shelters like those pictured in the photograph are located in Taos, New Mexico.

New Hampshire winter. Frude made it as plain as he could that cold really wasn't.

The instructor in such matters of the other of us at Governor Dummer Academy said it was the same with black and white, which are not colors at all but their lack.

The same sort of shiver encountered during a desert night, although relatively less than ours in New England's northeastern hills, is as much a contrast. It can, and sometime does, bring occasionally fatal hypothermia to someone unprepared, too lightly clothed, and perhaps weakened by the previous afternoon's sun burning through a tan in the skin-searing heat.

The Tropical Animals We Really Are

We actually are tropical animals able to survive in cold climates, though it's really here that we are more productive and efficient. Our ingenuity enables us to maintain our body temperatures within the physical limits set by our systems; to do this, we must ourselves constantly produce heat.

Our body heat comes from only two general sources: our food, which in survival conditions may be severely restricted; and from absorption of radiant energy from the day's sun and the night's lone campfire. There is an important ratio between your available food and your extent of activity.

We must ourselves continually produce heat, while ridding ourselves of enough to keep our own temperature constant. Such transfer of heat is accomplished by radiation, conduction, convection, and evaporation.

Radiation

When the outside temperature is colder than we, radiation losses account for about one-twentieth of our total depletion. Yet the only heat that can be lost by radiation is that which reaches the outermost layer of clothing or other covering. The higher the temperature of the radiating surface, the more rapid will be the heat loss. The energy lost to the body this way is an emission from the body itself. A layer of clothes tends to absorb the emission. It also tends to absorb or reflect the radiation from the sun or campfire and thus shield the body from energy gains.

Conduction is what occurs when we sit on a hot rock. The heat is passed from the substance of the rock to that of the body, rapidly because of the direct and firm contact. The greater the temperature difference, the more rapid and thorough the transfer. To avoid heat gain in the desert, you should walk on the hot ground with your feet well shielded.

Convection

Convection currents occur around the body where air molecules are heated and set up small air currents. Hot air is lighter than cold air, with hot and moist air being lighter than hot and dry air. The former also holds the warmth longer. These various heats tend to rise and swirl around the body under its covering until they reach an opening and pass into the open air.

Inasmuch as heat rushes from hot things to those which are cold, and since the greater the temperature differential the faster the flow, the sole way to protect your body from gain or loss is to separate or shield it with protective material, whether it is a tent or the clothes on your back.

A nonconductive layer is one that when heated on one side remains cool on the other. Still air, in the down of sleeping bags or in the weave of cloth, is the most common nonconductive material, and it can keep you warm or cool appropriately. The freely circulating air reflects the sum of its radiation-conduction-convection mix, however, and may be hotter than the body.

Desert Garb

The temperature of the skin tends to be around 92° Fahrenheit (33.5° centigrade). In the desert, the air is often a great deal hotter than that. The clothes are worn for protection against heat, sunburn, insects, blowing sand, and vegetation.

If you keep your head and body covered during the day, you'll survive longer on less water. Long trousers and shirts with the sleeves rolled down are a good idea. Keeping them loose and flapping will keep you cooler. Even on the desert, a light woolen shirt in your pack is not out of place. Pulled on when resting or when desert storms threaten, it can prove comfortable in preventing the rapid chilling that evaporation of perspiration sometimes brings about.

Wearing a cloth neckpiece to cover the back of your neck can help protect it from too much sun. A headpiece like that worn by the Arabs works better than a hat. A parachute can be adapted as a light and portable sunshade. Even a parasol makes sense. During dust storms, cover the mouth and nose with a cloth or kerchief.

The Layering Way

Shedding layers of clothing as you warm up, thereby always staying moderately cool, works well in the wide range of temperatures found in a day in the desert. This ability to gauge and maintain a comfortable body temperature increases markedly with experience.

Many find the layer system preferable everywhere in the farther places. In the chill of the morning, which actually deepens as the sun rises because of the breezes stirred by the lifting warmth, many like to start out with everything on. Whether you are on a winter desert or high in mountainous reaches, the practice is to continue shedding layers as the sun and its heat climb.

There is one thing to watch out for with such a system, and that is not to carry it too far. In the clear desert air, the sun burns deeply, even through a basic swimming pool tan. The shoulders and back, so critical if you backpack, are particularly vulnerable.

Evaporation

The evaporation of water accounts for the other 25 or so percent of heat loss from the body. Heat is lost from the body when perspiration is generated and passes to the surface to evaporate, helping to preserve the body's narrow range of suitable temperatures.

There are several other and lesser ways to lose heat by the evaporating water route. Dampness comes from the skin cells themselves to a very minor extent, and when we breathe, the air from our lungs with its warmth and wetness carries heat away.

Under the most severe circumstances, you can put out a gallon of sweat in an hour, a pace the body can not continue for very long. There is no way to adapt to water loss. If you are going to sweat, you must replace the lost water to maintain a normal range of temperature. You must have water.

Trying to Circumvent Frying

People who have lived and worked outdoors in the desert all their lives subconsciously move from shade to shade. Their paces are slow and rhythmic and, as they have found to be better, their clothing remains on. Staying away from the hotter spots they realize is important.

One of us became rather intimately concerned with heat stroke upon venturing onto the Red Wall in the Grand Canyon one hot afternoon. Fortunately, night and the Thunder River happily were soon in coming. Orienting your body toward the sun, it so proved, may help in a situation where no other substantial plus is available.

Then there is the convective cooling to be generated by fanning, moving into a breeze, or sitting in a draft. And it is well not to forget even momentarily that hot air carries its own penalties in terms of heat load as well as water consumption.

Getting Warm Without Getting Up

Inactivity reduces heat production to a minimum, and may offer at the time the most effective means of reducing the need to get rid of heat. In the cold desert night, to move to the other side of the scale, doing isometric exercises while in your sleeping bag can keep you warm. Shivering does the same thing without conscious effort.

Suppose you wake up cold, and you're too sleepy to bother with that campfire you were too weary to set up before turning in. Then either shivering or muscular tension exercises, when you merely strain one muscle against another, will warm you even more efficiently than if you had risen and chopped some wood.

With such external activity by axe, only a portion of the expended energy is realized as body heat. The rest is lost to the surrounding cold. When you lie in your mummy bag and strain one muscle against another for ten or fifteen minutes, nearly all the heat thus generated warms the body immediately and directly.

Another way to warm yourself is to eat something.

Shelter

A rectangle of light plastic, large enough to roof and thus waterproof a lean-to, can be folded and carried in a breast pocket as easily as a handkerchief. For years one of us has always carried an eight-by-twelve-foot plastic sheet, though its major use has been as a rainy-day shelter while toasting the noontime sandwich.

By the same criterion, the parachute silk that was once common ensures excellent lean-to covering, as it formerly did for downed military airmen during hostilities. This silk, sometime ago replaced by synthetics that lack that certain luxurious softness, can be used alone, although a corollary sheath of any suitable local vegetation that is at hand for the gathering makes it better.

Which should go underneath? Light-colored manufactured products, used directly atop an erected framework, will cheerily reflect brightness and warmth. Fabric beneath and browse above, therefore, can be the warmest response to a snapping cold night.

Plane Protection

The sufficiently intact fuselage, wing, and tail portions of a plane downed in desert country frequently can be turned into a functional shelter.

In the often year-round snow of rimming mountains, a main concern may be the fumes and flammability of spilled fuel. The fueslage, as is, can be inappropriate as a shelter because of the rapidity with which the metal could conduct away what little heat could be contrived. In the flat of the desert, on the other hand, the inside of the airplane's interior may be far too warm during the day. Then there's the shade of a wing to seek temporarily if you have no better shelter.

When you intend to stay with the plane, a shady and functional shelter can be fashioned by tying an opened parachute to a wing as an awning. Then, using sections of the plane tubing for poles and pegs, fasten the lower edge of the chute at least two feet clear of the sand for air circulation. Make sure, certainly, that the plane is staunchly moored and the wing securely guyed to withstand movement in wind or storm.

During the winter, particularly during the hours of darkness, desert temperatures may get below freezing, and hail and heavy rains fall. Then the plane's interior can be used for shelter from cold and wet. Cooking outside, though, may be advisable even when there is no danger from spilled gas if the accumulation of carbon monoxide could be a menace.

If you have a parachute or other suitable fabric, dig out a depression and cover it, always leaving some conspicuous sign of occupancy outside. In rocky regions or where desert shrub, thorn shrub, or tufted grass hummocks grow, a parachute, blanket, or sheet of plastic draped over such a protuberance could do.

Look for natural desert features such as an oasis tree, a rock cairn, or a tall clump of cacti for shelter or shade. Although the overhanging bank of a dry stream may offer a tempting retreat, a distant cloudburst could abruptly flood it. In safer country, the banks of valleys, dry rivers, and ravines are especially promising places to look for caves, and there's also the possibility of encountering some deserted native shelter.

Travel by Night

The main objective in the desert during the hot seasons will be to keep cool and thus conserve as much body moisture as possible, so traveling at night and bivouacing during the day may be the best procedure.

It's a matter of weighing the water need against the heat price. In the open sunlight, you gain some 150 calories of radiant energy per hour from direct radiation, the same from secondary radiation, and about an equal amount from conduction and convection. Add to this a variable amount from your own energy output. At rest, you require under a quart of water an hour. Add activity, and you will need much more. Look, therefore, for the most energy-efficient shelter first.

The shelter that you make should be cool during the day and warm during the night. A larger shelter is cooler in the day, creating a larger island of insulation. On the other hand, this same size is much harder to heat at night, when the source of warmth is your body. One solution is to use your space blanket, tarp, or chute as an awning during the day, then wrap it around your clothed body at night.

Then there's the warm companionship of a small, bright fire.

Coolest When It's Hottest

Ordinarily, when water is particularly limited, it's well to stay in whatever shade, contrived or otherwise, there may be during the hotter hours. The Department of Defense has found that the temperature at the bottom of a narrow trench scooped several feet deep (invaluable if it doesn't take too much sweat), can be over 80 degrees cooler than the desert surface.

Precisely, to be as cool as practical, such a slit should be aligned with where the sun rises and sets over flat equatorial desert on the two annual equinoxes. These arrive approximately March 21 and September 23, when the equator bisects the sun's center, and when both the day and night are twelve hours long.

Roughly, on the other hand, a slit running east and west at midday by local standard time, will be just about a maximum heat-excluding right angle to the sun's most searing rays.

9

Driving in the Desert

Sweltering in steel headgear and chest pieces, Coronado and his column of horsemen somehow toughed it through these southwestern deserts, past the Grand Canyon, on to Kansas and just about everywhere in between.

Always only a few miles further were the fabled Seven Cities of Cibola, which they believed must be more dazzling than the sun that pressed its heat on their backs. There, the story was, even the roads were cobbled with gold.

They found, from 1540 to 1542, only the Indian pueblos. But Francisco Vasquez de Coronado and his fellow seekers of golden El Dorado then stamped this land with an enduring culture whose grandeur still marks this country with ancient Spanish elegance. They also showed how long and how far human beings with a purpose can travel in heat unrelieved by air conditioning.

---

opposite page: There are more horses in the Southwest now than in the recognized heyday of these friends to man.

More Horses Than in Wild West Years

If you come from the temperate Northeast or even one of the central states, you'll find yourself absorbing some differences in life-style, in our cases with the enjoyable expectancy there can be in hurdling new challenges. One is apt to be the not-unexpected discovery that your aging car, designed for cold winters and only occasional hot summer days, may have certain lacks in such new intensity of sunlight.

Instead of salt and rust, here now are heat, dust, and relatively immense distances. The popular vehicles you'll now encounter will likely be a different breed from what you arrived driving, with unfamiliar modifications and accessories to consider.

Unlike what Coronado and Cabeza de Vaca made do with, modes of travel today are mostly mechanized. Even the majority of cowboys have been replacing their horses with pickups and jeeps. There are more horses in the Southwest now than in the recognized heyday of these friends to man. Now, though, they get hauled around in their own trailers from one jumping-off place to another. In getting from one place to another these days, the internal and sometimes infernal combustion engine is king.

All the Bicycles

There is one machine that is not dependent upon fossil fuels— the bicycle. Its popularity is still soaring. The young get around on rough-tired versions of the cross-county motorcycle. The elder generation more often relies on three-wheelers whose principal accessory is a huge basket for carrying groceries.

With the in-between ages, the ten-speed bicycle reigns. There are also the three-speeds and five-speeds, and, for the racers, the fifteen-speed bikes can pass them all. Prevailing on the bike trails, however, are those ten-speeds. They can be bought reasonably.

For the more exacting, local builders turn out custom models as advanced as the racing Ferrari is in its class, with accelerated prices to match. The basic physical requirement is a relatively intact cardiovascular and respiratory system in moderately good repair. You can get up to forty or more miles per hour on some of the custom vehicles, and there are recognized hundred-mile jaunts all over.

A cross-breed with some utility in the city, suburbs being uncommon in these abrupt expanses, is the moped. This moderately priced motorcycle with turning pedals gets gas mileage that may take a while to believe and nearly satisfying speeds. It lacks the speed and power of a true motorcycle and is not as good for physical conditioning as a bicycle. The moped's appeal perhaps lies in this rather bland image.

The genuine motorcycles can be right at home out here. They come in a considerable variety of sizes, powers, and images. There is the large, touring Harley Davidson type with the top-hat-and-tails elegance of saddlebags, fairings, matching boxes, and radios that certainly cost as much as their equivalents in a car.

They can cruise along at paces well in excess of present limits. They frequently evoke the riders' desire for matching attire, and in general this yen is expressed in pretty classy outfits.

The tough-guy image of the easy rider bikes can also be seen. Not infrequently, such motorcyclists can become pretty rugged customers. Most of their bikes are custom-made, often by their riders, with style sometimes being given more importance than sound engineering. Some such vehicles verge on being two- or three-wheeled cars.

Winter in Another World

The foreign machines, particularly those made by the Japanese, seem to dominate the lightweight to medium-weight bikes here where there's seldom snow to complicate riding. These are usually dependable, utilitarian vehicles, built to give top gas mileage at a low initial cost.

Then there are the lean, stripped bikes with knobby tires that climb hills and loop around race courses. Indeed, these are really racing bikes, and they are mimicked among some of the younger persons by bicycle races in the same style.

With the mandatory helmet law being voted out in Arizona, at least, the expected rise in head injuries has followed. The very obvious mobility of bikes with and without motors trends toward accidents. Even when the bike rider is behaving in an exemplary fashion, the automobile driver may not see him. The result is a bent or broken bicyclist, regardless of whose fault it may be.

A pedal-powered acquaintance commented that to survive, one had to act as if he or she were a Cadillac. Another relates hair-raising stories of near misses with pickups.

Dodging the Dehydration Danger

In the desert all the problems of heat load associated with the rapid flow of air warmer than the body, and of the therefore heightening evaporation of body moisture, result in high heat gain and high water loss, with the bicyclist's scant sensation of either.

Bikers need to make every effort to carry and drink plenty of fluids. Otherwise, the combination of light clothing, heavy radiant and convective gains, and exorbitant fluid loss can lead to collapse among the unwary.

The Almost Cars

Some peculiar *almost* cars are the ATCs and the ATVs. The former is a large-tired, three-wheeled motorcycle type of machine designed for rambling over rough country, depicted in motion pictures such as those portraying the 007 image of Ian Fleming's James Bond. Such machines tend to scar the countryside and provoke controversy about where, when, and how they should be used once they've been hauled to their take-off points, usually in a pickup or trailer.

Their construction, based on a triangle, is inherently less stable than that structured on a rectangle. The size of the tires, though, seems to stabilize the whole.

The ATVs double the action with six wheels. These minitanks seem to be able to go almost anywhere and over just about anything whose surface gives them traction. Not particularly fast, they act somewhat as a warm-weather breed of snowmobile. Though so far they have not proved to be stand-ins for the burro, the mule, and the amiable horse for back-country packing, there are outfitters hereabout asking one another, "Who knows what is coming next?"

Inland Dune Buggies

Another odd-looking vehicle is the dune buggy. These generally are built on VW engines and really consist of little more than the actual slung and unslung parts needed to move the car. Often their frames have large, smooth rear tires and lighter front tires.

Some are made up with the required lights, windshields, and so on that make them street-legal. They thrive in washes and amid sand dunes. The result is not without hazard. High-speed collisions and rolls occur too often. Bright little flags on the tips of high-antennae flutter there to increase awareness of their presence.

These dune buggies have the habit of churning up clouds of dust. So with them, too, opinions conflict about what may be their proper and improper place in desert living.

Motor Homes and Pickup Campers

True matches for the motorized yacht on big water are the motor home and the pickup camper on terra firma. Motor homes have an inherent philosophy that culminates very often in spaciousness. They dare the winds with relatively high profiles. They require the good roads favored by those who prefer to travel in comfort to places other tourists venture, such as national parks.

They have all the complications of the modern transoceanic power cruisers, including stoves, refrigerators, air conditioning, self-contained toilets, and the generators therefore that are needed. Desirably accompanying all this is the knowledge of how to keep all these functioning in a pinch, or at least how to have ready access to understandable information when away from major population centers.

The cab-over pickup campers are favored by acquaintances who travel to hunt or fish. Although they have some of the drawbacks of the motor home, such as high profiles, the pickups' underpinning encourages escaping paved roads. There's particular freedom inherent in the four-wheel drives, as with such three-quarter-ton pickups.

Equipment is available for leveling the camper, even for sliding it off the pickup, liberating this nucleus for use as a truck. This is a totally different assemblage from the easily detached pickup shell so handy for fishing, hunting, exploring, and prospecting—as much a part of today's canyon and desert country as the saguaro cactus and cowboy hat.

The Plus of the Front-Wheel Drive

An advantage of a front-wheel drive is that the engine and the transaxle, axle, transmission, and differential combined sit on top of the driving wheels. This makes for surer traction in slippery, rough, and steep going.

The front wheels pull the rest of the car around the corners, a reason why this arrangement used to be popular with the incline-climbing racers. The weight and the tunnel of the drive train are lessened, adding muscle to the power-to-weight ratio.

The Power Steering Story

With power steering, the resistance of the driving wheels is not very noticeable. An increasing number of cars are being built to this configuration, despite some problems. One is that with the power and the weight in front, this type of vehicle has a tendency to jump from understeer to oversteer suddenly if power is applied without this in mind.

More critical, in terms of money as well as time, if anything goes wrong in the power train or engine, the whole has to be dismantled for repairs. Also making for expensive mechanics' bills is that with the soaring use of plastic parts, the odds are that some clutch or transmission work will be necessary.

The Shade Tree Mechanics

With the front engine and rear drive setup, there would seem to be room for the already front-heavy vehicle to be better balanced. Pickup rear ends are notoriously light without a load. For shade tree mechanics, they are easier to work on with the parts spread out along the bottom. Despite everything, the devotees maintain, one becomes accustomed to all this, which puts familiarity on the user's side.

A limited-slip differential that helps to boost traction is available in some pickups. The theory is that when one wheel begins to spin, it can only turn a few revolutions before the gearing actually forces power to the other wheel, not a bad arrangement on muddy back roads.

The next step is power to all four wheels, whether all the time or with a lock-out. Some studies indicate a need for four-wheel traction some 10 percent of the time for the average buyer of four-wheel drives. Whether or not one really needs it depends upon how the truck is to be used.

After all, it is only recently that tractors have come to have four-wheel drive, and their job is to pull loads. Nonetheless, these trucks are very popular despite declines in gas or diesel mileage. Jeeps even have a differential lock that makes all four wheels spin together in the low range. We have found its pulling power awesome.

Such Drives Special Place

Four-wheel drives have had their own special place in America's collective heart ever since the jeep of World War II, some version of this vehicle having afterwards been made in country after country, many of them eventually reaching this country's roads. Jeeps themselves have developed into a whole family of vehicles, and there are related automobiles, as distinct from trucks.

The British Land Rover is occasionally seen roaming the countryside. The Toyota Land Cruiser is common. One of us has an old Cherokee with a full-time four-wheel drive; this with two ranges, automatic transmission, and the differential lock. Most of the time, the high range is all that is necessary to get there.

Transmissions

A four-speed transmission makes for less wear on the brakes, along with better control over rough spots and down steep trails. The automatic transmission, though, has never let us down. Maybe we just like to shift.

We had an old 1948 CJ2A, which was smaller than the current CJ model, and we are inclined to think that it was a bit handier off the road than the present size. At one time, Suzuki made one with similar dimensions, but it seems to have gone off the market.

One thing to assess, whether going domestic or foreign, is the availability of parts and repairs. If you're going off-road, you may well need both. In fact, some extras such as skid plates underneath and radiator guards make good sense. Saddle gas tanks to increase your range may also help.

Utility or Cosmetic

Extra quartz lights and spotlights can be useful, but they too often become part of the dressing most of the time. Two spare tires make sense if you are really going to utilize the vehicle's full potential. Don't forget the water!

There is a tremendous amount of heat generated by the sun on the road and the friction inherent in the car. To protect the engine, the biggest radiator that will fit is none too big; most gasoline engines today are designed to run hotter than of yore. For reasons of fluid flow and control at cooler moments, keeping the thermostat in the circuit is ordinarily a good idea.

In special situations, a thermostat that opens at a slightly lower temperature may be an improvement. In general, though, it is sounder to go with a large radiator capacity and stay with the standard thermostat. Most domestic manufacturers have so-called desert packages that *should* already be in a car you buy in the Southwest. If your vehicle is still the one that you brought to the desert country, it may need modifications.

If you are going to pull heavy loads such as trailers, a transmission cooler can be a good idea. If your transmission is not equipped with a cooler and you do not intend to modify it, you should make frequent checks to make sure that the fluid level is kept up.

Energy Drags

The drag of air conditioning used to eat up as much as 40 percent of usable power. Now it averages quite a bit less, and most late-model units have a cut-off feature when maximum engine load is required. If your unit does not have the cut-off feature, one may be added rather inexpensively. Part of the answer used to be a bigger engine, but with present fuel expense, the most reasonable way to prevent overheating is to give the cooling more muscle.

Above 45 miles per hour, the friction created by opening the windows can take more energy output then the air conditioning itself demands. At higher speeds, this is more noticeable. In some of today's bigger vehicles, such as the Suburbans or vans, it may take a front and a rear air conditioner, or roof type, to get the temperature down.

One way to cut down on the heat inside the car is to put reflective tinting or even one-way screens over the windows themselves (but *not* the windshield). These work. However, they do diminish vision at night on both sides and at the back. Frequently a compromise has to be accepted, otherwise the rear of some station wagons can become unbearable.

Choices and Whys

The choice of cooler, lighter colors for the automobile makes good sense. Greens do not stand up to the sun very well, but hot colors and dark colors are just that. It may be a type of conformity, but creams, yellows, grays, and white usually work out well overall, especially as these hues reflect a lot of heat that otherwise would be absorbed.

Choosing seat fabrics with an eye to heat is also wise. The velour type of materials allow a little cooling, and there are special cushions available to use during hot weather. The hard vinyl finishes are better avoided. Real lamb's wool works best in both heat and cold.

As far as maintenance is concerned, it is far less expensive in the long run to go a little overboard than to try to stretch the intervals between servicings. Sand, dust, and heat eat up oil. It should be changed even more frequently if you drive on dirt a lot. Many manufacturers are touting service schedules of seventy-five hundred miles or even more between changes. We are inclined to change the oil and the oil filter about every three thousand miles, but then we both drive on dirt a lot. Filter systems need to be checked, and the filters themselves replaced, at every oil change or as indicated by their condition.

Catalytic Converter Dangers

The emission control system has replaced the electrical system as the thing most likely to be out of whack in today's cars. PCV (Positive Crankcase Ventilation) valves and EGR (Exhaust Gas Recycling) valves take watching. They can make a car run hot and bring your fuel mileage down. Obstruction to the outflow tract, the exhaust system, can cause persistent high engine temperatures. The catalytic converter should be considered in the event of any such problems on the highways.

The catalytic converter is very dangerous in off-road driving. A by-pass may be installed, and often should be, to sidestep possible law problems. Where legal, the converter may be removed and a test tube extension may be used in its place.

One practice that will go a long way toward keeping you out of trouble is regular maintenance and periodic checking, especially of parts and places that are especially vulnerable. That is really a recurrent theme. It's only common sense to set up an all-over check in advance of any back-road trips where automotive disabilities can turn into human danger.

The Citizen Bands

A lot of people carry short-range citizen band radios in this part of the world where flat terrain and quality equipment can put you in touch with other travelers as far away as five to twenty-five miles. Individuals in a lot of desert country monitor certain channels and will help a traveler in need. One available unit plugs into the cigarette lighter and uses car battery current, has a removable antenna, and stores in a small case that can be kept handy.

A spare battery setup should be included. There is a switching circuit that allows it and the battery in use to be kept charged from the regular charging system. It also isolates either battery, so that one battery always remains fully charged. Also, if you drive at night, you will need a light for any repairs.

They used to say that this is hard country on men and horses. The same is true of cars. A little thought in trying to match the vehicle to its uses and a lot of thought in front of backcountry travel can go a long way to keeping that pleasure jaunt just that. We really are a nation dependent upon our vehicles. Taking care of yours only makes good common sense.

Tumbleweeds

Winds pull dry tumbleweeds from their roots and roll them across the countryside. These harmless, light masses of small, brittle stems are not themselves hazardous to traffic. Evasive steering to avoid tumbleweeds, though, can cause unwarranted collisions.

The Spectacular Dust

It's when the cloud formations of the thunderheads build up on hot summer afternoons that, in some areas, the desert's dust storms most often blur the heightening winds. Then likely comes the brief burst of cleansing rain.

Motorists familiar with such momentary traffic-blanketing turbulence reduce speed and turn on driving lights, leaving any freeways at exit ramps if possible. If dust becomes so intense they no longer can see for even the length of a football field, they pull off roadways, switch off driving lights, and turn on emergency flashers instead.

Only when visibility clears do they continue on their way, staying ready to move once more to where they can safely wait out any returning dimness if particles are again so swept up from the desert floor.

10

Keeping Your Backpack Lean

It is said that the joys of backpacking are half anticipation and half remembrance, and, somewhere in between, the actual doing. For whatever reason, once you start you keep coming back. The aches and twinges of the trip before ease away swiftly. Even a rock that intruded on a night's sleep no longer seems disagreeable.

It doesn't cost much to get started, and backpacking is an almost-perfect antidote for the claustrophobia of crowded living. Open country beckons in every part of our southwestern deserts. No special skills are required. In a certain sense, such travel takes you back to the days of striving to survive. It demands the major portion of your energies much of the time, leaving no time for the routine problems and concerns. And it is enjoyable.

North America today is such a vastly changed place. The economic stranglehold, the spreading urbanization, and the increasing dependence upon machines alone are confining enough. But there's the lessening importance of the very essence of what it was that

---

opposite page: Sharing breakfast grub with friends in the untroubled space on the desert's rim

first opened our frontiers—the pride and recognition embodied in individual effort.

Yet most of us find the chance for freedom elsewhere, as in today's increasing mobility and the additional leisure in which to enjoy it (these more a result of such changes than anything else). It is in this setting that we are witnessing a boom in outdoor activities by these same city dwellers. Part of that breaking away is the phenomenal growth of backpacking.

Heavy Boots and Satin Slippers

"Hiking a ridge, a meadow, a river bottom, is as healthy a form of exercise as one can get," said Supreme Court Justice William O. Douglas, with all the authority of a lifetime of personal experience. "Hiking seems to put all the body cells back into rhythm. Ten to twenty miles on a trail puts one to bed with his cares unraveled.

"Hiking—and climbing, too—are man's most natural exercises. They introduce him again to the wonders of nature, and teach him the beauty. . . . They also teach him how to take care of himself and his neighbors in times of adversity. We need exercise as individuals. We need to keep physically fit and alert as people. . . .

" 'History is the sound of heavy boots going upstairs and the rustle of satin slippers coming down.' Nations that are soft and sleek—people who get all their exercise and athletics vicariously—will not survive when the competition is severe and adversity is at hand. It is imperative that America stay fit. For today we face as great a danger, as fearsome a risk, as any people in history."

The Elements of Adventure

There are elements that go into planning and equipping an adventure that come out of the boots on your feet and the pack on your back, especially with a hike that lasts more than just the day and perhaps even more than just overnight. When you begin your plans for such efforts, the first and indeed the final consideration is weight.

Increasingly apparent on long hikes especially, every single inert item you take, whether used or not, you yourself must lug. The less each weighs, the lighter your pack or the more items you can bring.

In dry country hiking, when it is feasible, ordinarily you go from source of water to source of water. When you must carry what you drink, there's the consideration that slightly more than a quart of water itself weighs over two pounds. Without including the variables that containers involve, this figures out to nine pounds per gallon. One of us personally carries five quarts. You can make a dry camp, but if you do, there's the plaguing fact that the next day, in normal circumstances, you should reach water early.

Backpacking the way it can be done imposes no drudgery or hardships. There is nothing hard about it. You wander free and unfettered, with just enough easy exercise in the pure air to make the life thoroughly enjoyable, and with so much hearty and healthy pleasure that one day you realize such excursions, year after year, have become a happily anticipated habit.

Pleasures for Pennies

Carrying everything you'll need and traveling and camping where you will in unfrequented wilderness, or along hiking trails, or in the empty stretches that are nearest is one of the most rewarding ways of sojourning in the open. Coupled with it are two advantages over otherwise vacationing afield.

Bringing water or keeping in its vicinity, you are footloose and free to roam, pitch your shelter where you will, or bed down under Orion's belted brightness. Gone is any necessity to depend on anyone but yourself. There's not even the expense and nuisance of cars or burros.

No vacationing on your own is less costly. Once you have reached the jumping-off place you've chosen, your compact and inexpensive rigging packed and ready, ahead is exploring and hunting and prospecting at no further expense other than for whatever food you don't forage on your own.

Who, You?

Backpacking trips are by no means limited to the husky young. Anyone fairly healthy and vigorous is eligible. Backpacking can be equally enjoyed by men and by women—by young people and by the older who also find joy outdoors.

In fact, one of the hikers who has traversed the entire two thousand and fifty miles of the Appalachian Trail *in a single year* was a gentleman seventy years old—George F. Miller of Washington, D. C. He covered every foot of it in 1952, carrying his pack and camping out most nights. At the other extreme, parents do commonly take their little tots along.

Those who have adapted themselves to the most functional methods of backpacking keep getting back outdoors and bringing others with them. They frequently combine the satisfactions of hiking and camping with fishing in the high waters of still-primitive wilderness, all at little if any more expense than it would cost to live at home.

Individualism in a Crowd

Backpacking's popularity, as with the desert itself, seems to be generating its own problems—problems which are by-products of civilization. The country is large but not without limit. Hiking on the heels of the backpacker ahead, as can happen when throngs keep returning to the same popularized trails, does not enhance one's oft-sought real wilderness experience.

Because of this, and even more detracting, the trappings of regulated existence are showing up in what used to be backcountry: "Camp only in designated areas," "Camping by permit only," and other such turnoffs. Maybe the days before these regulations existed generate a bit of nostalgia, but be that as it may, unfortunately, that's the way it is now in some places.

This is not only a problem of backpacking. Downhill skiing has been trying to cope with crowds for much longer, and the sport itself continues to be a pleasurable experience. Perhaps a way will be found for the hordes to retain the essence of the backpacking experience and yet keep it a credible activity still available to those who wish to participate.

The In and Out of It

No more American frontier? A still-not-surveyed 383 million acres of our country, 17 percent of the United States, is in the West.

Great natural wonders like the Leviathan Cave in Nevada were discovered only a handful of years ago.

You, we, and every other American own together a whooping one-third of all this country's land, a large portion of it hereabout. Close to half of Utah and Nevada are included in just the American government's nearly 800 million acres.

On top of that there is what our individual states, municipalities, and other public jurisdictions themselves possess. As an example, only 18 percent of Arizona, whose 113,909 square miles make it the sixth largest state in the nation, is privately owned.

There's so much room for backpacking in this country that some of the more eager hikers have developed a way to cram more into their lifetimes. They have an outfitter pack or fly their duffle to where they can camp more or less permanently in some favorably situated locality and return to bring them out on a prearranged date. In the meantime, they can be exploring the region with only light loads.

The country is so vast and open in these four desert-enhanced states, and in most areas the scenery is so generously varied and grand, that you can easily spend a month or more taking short trips to and from an established camp and never exhaust the possibilities for variety and enjoyment.

Clover, Grass, and Clean Earth

"Any backpacker can do worse than copy the woodchuck who is one of our cleanest animals, although most unjustly called a groundhog," Colonel Townsend Whelen often noted. "His burrow never smells of anything but clover, grass, and clean earth. In it he has a blind alley, at the end of which he deposits all refuse and covers it with earth.

"Remember that you are camping in God's clean country. Leave it as pure and unspoiled as you found it, and do not make it look like Hell. Take good care of yourself, and take good care of the places where you pitch your shelter. You'll return home healthier, and you and those who follow you will always have fine places in which to kindle those never forgotten campfires."

All Roaming Is Divided into Three Parts

All roaming is divided into three parts: the anticipatory stir of getting ready, the actual adventure, and after it all, the deep-down pleasure of reminiscence.

Although you may not plan to hit the trail again for a month or a year, you will be missing some of the keenest joy of all if as soon as one journey is done, you do not start preparing for the next. You'll be letting get by you the heart-quickening satisfaction of keeping your gear ready, of purposefully fingering maps, and of crowding brief reminders into a worn memo book pocketed for those moments inspiration sparks.

Then once again, almost before you know it, the wilderness night begins bulging from the west in a deep blue flood that drenches all but the last few waning embers of the sunset. Sweet ebony fumes lift from ready kindling, and then the heavier aspen with its clean, medicinal bite catches hold.

By you, in the untroubled space on the desert's rim, is shelter, grub, nested aluminum cookware, cool-lipped steel cups, that telescoping rod just in case, and living warmth. Life is especially good.

Nothing is particularly new about hiking and camping with only what we can easily pack on our backs. Early frontiersmen traveled that way whenever they entered the wilderness. Daniel Boone spent two whole years more or less alone in Kentucky's then virgin wilds, living off the country, with no outfit except for what he had with him when taking to the bush.

Better equipment and improved methods have rid the pleasant pastime of backpacking of any drudgery or taxing work. These merit close, careful consideration by those who themselves may try the trail, based as they are on the most fundamental of experience. Those who have never done any backpacking or ventured into the silent places with only what they could carry are sometimes held back by the idea that it is the toughest kind of toil. Indeed, frequently heard from those tackling the sport without even a sound outfit are closed-minded declarations of having no intention of making pack animals of themselves again.

It is an unfortunate fact, particularly for the individuals involved, that some half of those who blunder through such a well-intentioned vacation never again give it a try because they have found it too much hard work, the direct result of wrong equipment and sadly inept technique.

The Pick of the Packs

One of the two packs especially well suited for this sort of vacationing is the alpine variety of frame rucksack, usually made with a single large and several smaller fabric compartments built around a strong, lightweight frame to which rugged shoulder straps are fastened.

The other is the long-satisfactory packboard, which goes back to prehistoric mankind. Basically, this is a rectangular frame over which fabric is so tightly doubled and laced that a bundle lashed to it never touches the wearer's back. Both are obtainable in a choice of sizes.

The best packs in the world for this type of recreation are actually American-made variations of the packboard. Light, strong, and durable, those today are often made of tough aluminum tubing, although such metals as magnesium and stainless steel are also used. Webbing, usually nylon, keeps all hard surfaces away from the hiker's spine.

Carrying bags, obtainable from the same outfitters and stores as the frames, fit these so that the result is utility, along with convenience and comfort. Anyone with plans to cover very many miles of backpacking, recreational or professional, would do well to consider very seriously making such a pack the basic part of his outfit. The wrong pack has ruined more vacations of this sort than any other single item.

Weighty Matters

The total weight of the loaded backpack, especially for travel higher than your attic, should not exceed some thirty-five pounds for the young and robust who take to the trails. This maximum should be trimmed to fifteen to twenty-five pounds for the less husky. As for proportioning, the equipment in the largest packs should not weigh over fifteen pounds, thus allowing a food and water load of twenty pounds at least.

Ample subsistence for one individual for one day can be contained within two and a quarter pounds of carefully selected and reasonably dehydrated foods. The 35-pound pack allows one to carry victuals enough for over eight days, not including the day going in and the day coming out.

Therefore, ten days on the average is the practical duration of a backpacking trek between sources of supply, except when rations are supplemented with wild edibles like fish and berries as one goes along. What can make the difference in the desert is having to carry your water.

A waist belt, weighing three ounces or so, usually is welcome when you are starting out with a heavier-than-usual pack, ordinarily helping both by stabilizing the load and by advantageously transferring some of the weight from the shoulders to the slope of the buttocks.

"It is some advantage to learn what are the necessaries," Thoreau found. "Most of the luxuries and many of the so-called comforts are not only dispensable but positive hindrances."

Staples in the Silent Spaces

Not much is more important when backpacking than the grub. Most of us go into the farther places to have a good time. If the victuals are poor, unwholesome, or not what we crave, we have a continuous grouch. If they are appetizing and there's plenty of everything, all is rosy. Satisfying victuals even make up for rain and hard beds. Good fellowship is at its best around good meals.

Now is not too soon to get started on your provisioning for that hike back of beyond. Done right, it's going to take some time. You'll do best to take foods you personally like and know how to prepare. Experimenting at home and on weekend journeys is the soundest way to determine how much of each item you'll need to round out the sort of satisfying meal that will keep you going under full power.

For that energy when it's required most, the quickest and most efficient source is the sugar in pastry, spaghetti, and breads. Along with such other agreeable energy suppliers as fresh and dried fruits, they ordinarily can be relied on for over half of one's entire caloric intake. The combination not only provides healthy amounts of what makes for get-up-and-go, but it comes with the minerals, vitamins, and fiber common among the nutritional essentials for prime performance.

With the higher amounts active backpackers eat, it is possible in some instances that additional thiamine may be called for, this being the particular B vitamin the human body uses in proportion to its intake of any carbohydrate. Some depletion of potassium, a factor in muscle cell function and fatigue, turns up occasionally if rarely in connection with the debilitating weakness sometimes overtaking an individual on the trail during unusually strenuous going. This can be an agreeable reason for trail-snacking on such delectable potassium sources as dried apricots.

Protein needs nowise increase with activity, though; the protein excesses too often heard of among professional athletes, the scientists conclude, being in fact much wiser and far safer avoided.

For Footing It

If you will examine the hooves of mountain sheep and goats, you will see that the outer rim of each hoof consists of a hard shell with a sharp edge where it contacts the ground. The interior of the hoof has a comparatively soft pad not unlike the consistency of crepe rubber. The entire foot is a fine example of how the sole of a safe mountain shoe should be constructed.

The proven favorites among most trail veterans, especially in the West, are the special boots—both imported and domestic—stocked by the big catalogue-issuing sporting-goods dealers for the express purpose of hiking. Equipped with the best of rubber lug soles, these afford high traction and long wear. They are safe, comfortable, and quiet, but not inexpensive. With reasonable care they are good for years, however, especially as they can be resoled.

For travel along the tamer trails in just what you have on, some of the new generation of running and jogging shoes work well. They are light, cool, readily available, and give practical support except for protection against turned ankles. They do not stop a cactus thorn very well, but then nothing short of fairly heavyweight hiking boots does.

The First Campfire

For camps where wood is available, we both ordinarily prefer the open blaze in conjunction with some sort of a lean-to shelter.

Such a campfire takes a part of everyone back to when our earliest ancestor cooked his meat for the first time and, rolled in furs, spent his initial night in a shallow cave warmed by the newly harnessed flicker of flame. It is the atavistic memory of this discovery, which lifted mankind above the lower animals, that is one of the chief urges drawing a lot of us back to the trails again and again.

The Rite of B'iling the Kittle

The backpacker who is already accustomed to far northern and particularly Canadian trails often must also sip his steaming cup of tea at noon here in the desert ridges, even if he has nothing to eat. This is almost a religion up under the aurora borealis, where it's known as *b'iling the kittle*.

Only a brief fire is needed, a mere handful of dry wood to flare up temporarily and swiftly disintegrate into ashes, a few specks of which invariably seem to swirl up to float unheeded in the dark brew.

Get the water bubbling. Drop in a roughly measured teaspoon of tea for every cup of water. Remove immediately from the heat to a safe place. Five minutes of steeping is enough.

The Stove Story

If open fires are out of the question, you'll likely need a backpacking stove. These come in a variety that at first seems bewildering. But there are basically two types, one using liquid fuel and the other bottled gas.

The one-burner primus stove is often the answer for hikers above the tree line. If you're in and out without any serious climbing, though, it may be more reasonable where you are going to pack a little wood instead. In any event, these light and efficient little stoves may be obtained in functional units using kerosene, gasoline, or canned gas.

Alcohol is not generally adequate, burning with too cool a flame.

Shelter by Poncho

A poncho handles foul weather well. Other times, some find it useful as a groundsheet, even a shelter and for other trail functions.

Worn during rain, it should be loose enough to permit welcome ventilation. Other times, as when the wind is wailing, such looseness can be a problem. Yet even then donning the poncho is very often preferable to encasing your body in closely fitting oilskins or other rainwear that can soon have you more uncomfortably soaked, this time with perspiration.

Knives for Pocket and Belt

A pocket knife with a single, thin, sturdy blade will indeed serve many purposes. But many of us discover, particularly during ultralight travel, that it is practical to add a sheath knife for the heavier tasks.

A light blade five or six inches long works well on the ridges and high slopes far back of beyond for slicing green boughs off where they angle vulnerably out of the trunk when a shelter is to be made, readying fish for the next meal, and for handling other such tasks. A substantial sheath, well reinforced at the tip, should be added for safety. If you don't want to carry it on your belt, it packs handily.

Although a good handcrafted trail knife is quite expensive, you get what you pay for. A Randall knife that has been dependable in some rather strenuous situations has a slim yet rugged, straight six-inch blade and a light, unbreakable, nonslipping handle in which is set a small, accurate compass. This can be one's emergency spare in case the regular compass becomes lost.

In a tough snap pocket sewn to the outside of the sheath is a little carborundum stone, with a medium grit on one side and a fine grit on the other, for keeping the blade sharp.

The Hiking Staff

An item that can be markedly practical on extended journeys is the hiking staff. Many of these here in the desert are fittingly self-made from the sturdy, tough, long, lightweight spines of dead saguaro cactus, soon exposed when the rest of its accordianlike length is stripped away by the west wind. Here also, where high mountains rear abruptly above the sands and catch the snows, are other homebred staffs, those scavenged from unmatched and discarded ski poles.

Personally favored is a folding unit of aluminum tubing, with a shock cord that springs into shape and holds the sections together. It is light, easily stowed away, and handy to carry.

Bamboo makes a nice stick. The Japanese fighting stick, the Bo, is supposed to reach from the floor to your armpit. The hiking stick can be that length or any other that feels right, something you find out for yourself by trial and error. In any event, such a hiking supplement has the makings of becoming unexpectedly useful in rough country, as a support when steadying helps, and on occasion just as a crutch to one's courage.

A hiking stick that takes into account that even in sere regions wet seasons come around may be a golf-type umbrella. For many, though, it's too short to become an everyday walking stick.

Perhaps part of such a suggestion is that though the practical is not always fashionable, it is always practical.

Down Jacket

A light down jacket is one of the more comfortable garments to draw on in the desert when you pause for the night, enthusiastic though relaxed and tired.

Much such country becomes suddenly cold when the sun sinks and the heat, with little moisture in the atmosphere to beat it back, disappears out of the sand and rocks.

In the somehow luminous dark when, after eating and tidying up, you laze in front of your small bright fire, the garment feels luxurious against your heretofore chilly back. Later, if your sleeping bag is the least bit cold, spread this same soft jacket between the robe and the mattress.

Optics

Anyone requiring prescription lenses to get around surely and safely is likely to argee that it will be only prudent to carry a spare pair in a substantial protective case. In the desert you would be wise to bring along a pair of optically correct and strongly constructed sunglasses.

Today's shatterproof and impact-resistant glasses are the ones, in any event, for the remote and faraway solitudes.

It's the Doing

These are the bold outlines of backpacking, one of the better antidotes when civilization starts to seem overwhelming. Each individual discovers the right combination of comfort and need that suits his purposes. Each will discover in his own way what parts he likes. And each will also find that the doing is everything.

11

Eating Off Desert Country

No stringent rules can be set down for survival anywhere, particularly in the drier places. Conditions, as well as situations, vary. So do localities. Especially do individuals. Initiative, on the other hand, may be guided by a consideration of general principles such as those we can here absorb.

Many of the pitfalls, too, may be so recognized and evaded, when they otherwise might have to be learned by unnecessarily hard and often dangerous personal experience. It will be far more satisfactory to deal with natural difficulties by adaptation and avoidance than by attempting to overcome them by force.

Using the ways of eating off the countryside considered herein as a foundation for ingenuity and common sense, anybody who suddenly finds himself dependent upon his own resources will have a better chance both to keep living and to walk away from any hardships smiling.

---

opposite page: The desert is too big to fight, but for those who can take advantage of what it freely offers, nature will furnish every necessity.

The desert is too big to fight. Yet for those of us able to take advantage of what it freely offers, nature will furnish every necessity including food.

Sustenance in the Sandy Spaces

Starvation is not a great deal more pleasant than most of us would expect. The body becomes auto-cannibalistic after a few foodless hours. The carbohydrates in the system are devoured first. The fats follow.

This might not be too disagreeable, inasmuch as reducing diets seek to accomplish much the same result, but then proteins from muscles and tendons are consumed to maintain dwindling strength. There is no need to explain why, if any of us are ever stranded and hungry in the wilderness, we will want to start when our strength is near its maximum not to pass up any promising sources of sustenance.

Few will disagree, at least not when the moment of decision is at hand, that there is a point where luxuries as such become relatively unimportant. One of those we esteem most highly is the freedom to indulge our taste prejudices. These taste prejudices, a better understanding of which may one day prove beneficial, are commonly based on two factors.

First: there is a human tendency to look down upon certain foods as being beneath one's social station. Where grouse have been particularly thick in the Northeast, we have seen them scorned among backwoodsmen as a "poor man's dish." The same season in the Northwest where there happened to be a scarcity of grouse but numerous varying hares, the former were esteemed while one heard habitants apologizing for having rabbits in their pots.

Second: it is natural to like the food to which we became accustomed. We in the United States and Canada have our wheat. The Mexican has his corn, the Oriental his rice. These grains we like also, but it would seem a hardship to have to eat them every day as we do wheat bread.

Fastidious, we are perhaps repelled by the idea of a Polynesian's eating raw fish, although at the moment we may be twirling a raw oyster in grated horseradish. The Eskimo enjoys fish mellowed by age. Many of us regard as choice some particularly moldy, odoriferous cheeses.

Letting Predators Hunt For Us

If one of us is ever stranded and hungry, it may not be amiss to watch for owls, for spying one roosting in a quiet shadowy spot is not unusual, and it may be possible to steal close enough to knock it down. Although not as large and plump as would seem from outward appearances, an owl nevertheless is excellent eating.

What is more likely, however, is that we may scare an owl from a kill and thus secure ourselves a fresh supper. We may also have such good fortune, perhaps earlier in the day, with other predatory birds such as hawks and eagles. It is not uncommon to come upon one of these which has just captured a jackrabbit or other prey that is proving awkward to lift from the ground, and by running nearer to drive the successful hunter away with its talons empty.

Can Live Meat Be Overheated

Wild coyotes and foxes may also be surprised at fresh kills that are still fit for human consumption. Such carnivores will seek new whereabouts at the sight or scent of an approaching human being.

One often hears it suggested that when any bird or animal has been unduly harassed before death, as may be considered to be the case if for example it has been relayed by predators, its meat is not fit to eat. Such conclusions, however commendable their interpretation, arise usually from fashion more than from fact, although it is true that the appreciable amounts of lactic acid in such tissues do increase the rate of spoilage.

But it was because of this very characteristic, the fact that acids released by such stimuli as prolonged fatigue and fright make meat more tender, that not so long ago it was an unpleasant custom of the civilized world to make sure that animals killed for their meat died neither swiftly nor easily when either could be prevented.

How About Bears

Coming up to a bear's kill in the higher rim country or back among surrounding ranges may be something else again. A wild bear probably won't dispute your presence. Then again it may, and although the chances are very much against this latter possibility, that is all the more reason not to take disproportionate risks.

If you are unarmed and really need the bear's meal, you will want to plan and execute your campaign with all reasonable caution. This will probably mean, first of all, spotting with the minutest detail preferably at least two paths of escape in case a fast exit should become advisable. This should not be too difficult where there are small trees to climb.

You'll then watch your opportunity and if, for instance, the kill is a still warm fawn perhaps build a large fire beside it, discreetly gathering enough fuel to last for several hours or until morning, if night be close at hand. You will take care in any event to be constantly alert until well away from the locality, realizing that bears, especially when they have gorged themselves, have a habit of dropping down near their food.

If you have a gun, you will be able to judge for yourself if the best procedure may not be to bag the bear itself. Fat for several reasons, later discussed, becomes the most important single item in most survival diets, and the bear is particularly well fortified with this throughout most of the year. Except usually for a short period in the spring, bear flesh is therefore particularly nourishing.

Many, most of whom have never tasted bear meat nor smelled it cooking, are prejudiced against the carnivore as a table delicacy for one reason or another. One excuse often heard concerns the animal's eating habits. Yet the most ravenous bear is a finicky diner when compared to such offerings as lobster and chicken.

It is only natural that preferences should vary, and if only for this reason it may be interesting to note:

(a) that many of our close acquaintances who live on wild meat much of the time relish plump bear more than any other North American game meat with the single exception of the desert and other sheep.

(b) and that, furthermore, these individuals include a sizable number who, after long professing an inability to stomach bear meat in any form, find themselves coming back for thirds and even fourths of bear roast or bear stew under the impression that anything so savory must be, at the very least, choice beef.

Getting Birds Without Guns

Birds promise feasts for anybody stranded or astray in wild country, especially as stones or such are often the only weapons needed. If one misses the first time, game birds in particular frequently afford a second and even a third try. When they do fly, they often go only short distances and may be productively followed, even more likely if this is done casually and at such a tangent that it would seem that one were going to stroll on past.

Although it goes without saying that no sportsman will find any amusement in indiscriminate killing, it follows with equal reason that under survival conditions when wild meat may mean life itself, such otherwise distasteful procedures will be justified by their success, even though regrets for their necessity may remain.

Any bird, as a matter of fact, will furnish good eating in an emergency. The only difference is that some are tenderer, plumper, and to different palates better flavored than others. Colonies afford particular opportunities. Even the riper eggs often obtainable should not be overlooked when one needs food.

Why Porcupines Are Given Reprieves

Porcupines, like thistles and nettles, are better eating than it might seem reasonable to expect. The slow moving, dull-witted rodent is in human estimation often a nuisance, being so ravenous for salt that practically anything touched by human hands will, whenever possible, be investigated by sharp inquisitive teeth.

When shooting the rocky headwaters of the Southwest Miramichi River in New Brunswick, one of us had to hunch out of his sleeping robe a half-dozen times a night to switch determined brown porkies away from his canvas canoe. Several years later, a sourdough told him how, when boating mail along the Peace and Finley in the Canadian Rockies, he'd solved with better success a similar problem, looping wires harmlessly around the yellowish necks of offending western hedgehogs and hitching them to poplars until he was ready to go the next morning.

The sluggish porcupine is the one animal that even the greenest tenderfoot, though weak with hunger, can kill with a weapon no more formidable than a stick. All one usually has to do thus to collect a meal is reach over the animal, which generally presents the raised quills of back and tail, and strike it on the head. Being so low in intelligence the hedgehog requires a lot more killing than might be expected.

Porcupines can not, of course, shoot their quills, but any that are stuck in the flesh by contact should be pulled out immediately, for their barbed tips cause them to be gradually worked in out of sight. This danger from quills is one reason why it is a poor practice to cook a porcupine by tossing it into a small fire. Very often all the quills are not burned off. Even if they are, a considerable amount of fat will no doubt be consumed as well.

The best procedure is to skin out the hedgehog, first turning it over so as to make the initial incision along the smooth underneath portion. Many who've dined on this meat consider the surprisingly large liver uncommonly toothsome.

The Most Widely Hunted Game Animal

In the spring, particularly those years when rabbit cycles are near their zeniths, the young lie so fearlessly that a dog will step over one without scenting it, and all an individual has to do, if he wants, is to reach down and pick the youngster up.

Adult rabbits themselves depend so much on camouflage that at any time if you pretend not to see one and continue strolling as if going past, it is frequently possible to come close enough to do some immediately accurate throwing with a ready stone.

Tularemia is occasionally a threat in some localities and in one respect the disease is a little harder to avoid when not hunting with a firearm, for one precaution can be to shoot only rabbits that appear to be lively and in good health. The germs of rabbit fever are destroyed by heat, however, and another safeguard is to handle the animal with covered hands until the meat is thoroughly cooked.

Rabbits are unusually easy to clean. One method you may already use is commenced by pinching up enough of the loose back skin to slit by shoving a knife through. Insert your fingers and tear the fragile skin apart completely around the rabbit. Now peal back the lower half like a glove, disjointing the tail when you come to it and finally cutting off each hind foot. Do the same thing with the top section of skin, loosening it finally by severing the head and two forefeet.

You can then, as you've very possibly found, pull the animal open just below the ribs and flip out the entrails, retrieving heart and liver. You may also want to cut out the small waxy gland between each front leg and the body.

Starvation Next To Impossible

"It is next to impossible to starve in a wilderness," noted George Leonard Herter, sporting goods manufacturer, importer, and exporter. "If no game, fish, mollusk, etc., are present, you are still in no danger.

"Insects are wonderful food, being mostly fat, and far more strengthening than either fish or meat. It does not take many insects to keep you fit. Do not be squeamish about eating insects, as it is entirely uncalled for. In parts of Mexico, the most nutritious flour is made from the eggs of small insects found in the marshes. In Japan, darning needles or dragon flies are a delicacy. They have a deliciously delicate taste, so be sure to try them.

"Moths, mayflies, in fact about all the insects found in the woods, are very palatable. The only ones I ever found that I did not care for were ants. They contain formic acid and have a bitter taste. A small light at night will get you all the insects you need to keep you in good condition. If the weather is too cold for flying insects, kick open some rotten logs or look under stones and get some grubs. They keep bears fat and healthy and will do the same for you."

In fact, only avoid one of insects' own enemies, toads.

Odd Meals

Grasshoppers are edible when hard portions such as wings and legs have been removed. So are cicadas. Termites, locusts, and crickets are similarly eaten.

Both lizards and snakes are not only digestible but are often considered delicacies for which some willingly pay many times the amount they expend for a similar weight of prime beef. The only time snake meat may be poisonous is when it has suffered a venomous bite, perhaps from its own fangs.

This also holds true with lizards, the only poisonous ones on this continent being the Southwest's Gila monster and Mexico's beaded lizard. To prepare the reptiles, decapitate, skin, remove the entrails, and cook like chicken to whose white meat the somewhat fibrous flesh is often compared.

Some aborigines have capitalized on the ants' acidity by mashing them in water sweetened with berries or sap to make a sort of lemonade. The eggs and the young of the ant are also eaten.

An ancient method for securing already cooked insects, reptiles, and small animals is to fire large tracts of grassland and then to comb them for whatever may have been roasted by the conflagration.

A Code For Survival

Although it is true that under ideal conditions the human body can sometimes fend off starvation for upwards of two months by living on its own tissues, it is equally certain that such auto-cannibalism is seldom necessary anywhere in the North American wilderness.

A good rule is not to pass up any reasonable food sources if we are ever in need. There are many dead men who, through ignorance or fastidiousness, did.

All this is perfectly distinct to an observant eye, and yet could easily pass unnoticed by most.

Next to last entry in Thoreau's
journal. September 3rd, 1861.

Other books by Bradford Angier

The Competence Factor
The Best of Colonel Townsend Whelen (with Colonel Townsend Whelen)
Bradford Angier's Backcountry Basics (edited by Esme Detweiler)
Home Cookbook of Wild Meat and Game
Camping-on-the-Go Cookery (with Zack Taylor)
Wilderness Neighbors
Ask for Love and They Give You Rice Pudding (with Barbara Corcoran)
Field Guide to Medicinal Wild Plants
Master Backwoodsman
Wilderness Wife (with Vena Angier)
Color Field Guide to Common Wild Edibles
The Freighter Travel Manual
Looking for Gold
Field Guide to Edible Wild Plants
Introduction to Canoeing (with Zack Taylor)
Survival with Style
Wilderness Gear You Can Make Yourself
One Acre and Security
Feasting Free on Wild Edibles
How to Live in the Woods on Pennies a Day
The Art and Science of Taking to the Woods (with C. B. Colby)
A Star to the North (with Barbara Corcoran)
Home Medical Handbook (with E. Russel Kodet, M.D.)
More Free-for-the-Eating Wild Foods
Being Your Own Wilderness Doctor (with E. Russel Kodet, M.D.)
Gourmet Cooking for Free (in paperback as Foods-from-the-Woods Cooking)
The Ghost of Spirit River (with Jeanne Dixon)
Skills for Taming the Wilds
Free for the Eating
Home in Your Pack
Mister Rifleman (with Colonel Townsend Whelen)
Living off the Country (in paperback as How to Stay Alive in the Woods)
How to Build Your Home in the Woods
At Home in the Woods (with Vena Angier)